Fearless Death

Buddhist Wisdom on the Art of Dying

Fearless Death

Buddhist Wisdom on the Art of Dying

Diamond Way Press is the publishing arm of the Buddhismus
Stiftung Diamantweg, a non-profit organization dedicated
to the preservation of Buddhist wisdom.

Buddhismus Stiftung Diamantweg
Dieburger Straße 148 A ı 64287 Darmstadt, Germany

Original Title in German: *Von Tod und Wiedergeburt*
Editor: Caty Hartung
English Translation: Pit and Maike Weigelt, with Kenn Maly

Scholarly Consultation: Kerstin Seifert, Manfred Seegers,
Michael Fuchs, Jim Rheingans, and Burkhard Scherer
Proofreading: Paul Partington, Jeri Masciocchi, Vicky Reeves
Cover and Book Design: Milla Kicilińska Gibson
Pictures and Graphics: Mika Blauensteiner
Cover Photo: Marcin J.Muchalski

International Standard Book Number
ISBN 13: 978-0-9752954-1-0
Library of Congress Control Number: 2012954291

Manufactured in the United States of America

Dedicated to the joyful cooperation
in Diamond Way.

CONTENTS

LAMA OLE NYDAHL

Fearless Death

Buddhist Wisdom on the Art of Dying

ACKNOWLEDGEMENT

I would like to thank everybody who helped with this book. Peter Speier collected my lectures on the topic and already in 1991 handed me a complete manuscript. Astrid Poier from Graz was able to compose a shorter summary of the teachings in 1993, but only after 2005 had the time come to focus on this book. The teachings were reinforced by the many questions during my Phowa courses, by experiences with students while dying, and by my own parachute accident.

My Caty, who is part of every success, accompanied the development of this book for the last two decades. Michael Fuchs and Pit and Maike Weigelt have been supporting us for the last five years. We owe Mika Blauensteiner thanks for the professional pictures and graphics. The extensive glossary has been carefully compiled again by Manfred Seegers, Jim Rheingans and Burkhard Scherer.

As usual, we were lovingly taken care of by our friends at our Europe Center, on Sardinia and in Graz, allowing us to use every moment to write.

I think many will join me in thanking them all.

PREFACE

....

When my wife Hannah found out that she had lung cancer, we were shocked, but inwardly calm. We knew what awaited us and especially her. Her mind stayed open, despite our strong love for each other. She used the last months of her life as well as possible to complete her work and then consciously said goodbye to all her friends, the day before she lost her speech. She died with dignity, a smile on her lips.

Since 1968, when Buddha's teachings had inspired us in Nepal, our skilled teachers had prepared us to help others in the dying process, and to help ourselves in our own dying. My wife needed no further teachings and used the appropriate meditations in full confidence. The people surrounding her could best adapt to her needs because they also knew what was important during that time, and in this way she was lovingly accompanied and supported during the process of dying.

The mourning period for Hannah also looked different from the usual. I continued to work, after a brief withdrawal, because I knew that she was much better off in her present state than in her sick body, and because I was sure we would joyfully continue our work together in future lives.

Trained according to the wishes of our lamas and their

transmission, over the years I became a teacher precisely for this decisive moment in life. With increasing joy, I can always observe what wholesome effect Buddha's teachings have on unsettled people who do not know what to expect at the end of their lives.

All students who know the teachings about the timeless mind, dying, death and rebirth, and in particular the practice of Conscious Dying *(Phowa)*, have one thing in common: They look fearlessly into the future, think of others, and are sources of strength for their surroundings. They are the quiet center of the storm that befalls the family when death is imminent.

May this book take away the fear of dying for many people and help them already now to plant the seeds for great future happiness!

Overlooking the lake and the mountains in the Europe Center in July, 2010, in the blessing-field of the Protectress White Umbrella, on the day of Black Coat,

Yours,
Lama Ole

THE CYCLE OF LIFE

Everything starts with the union of the largest and the smallest
cell in a human being: the egg of the woman and the sperm
of the man. From this merging, trillions of cells arise in two
hundred different manifestations within nine months. After one
month, an approximately six-millimeter-long being has evolved.
And four weeks later arms, legs, hands and feet appear. In the
process, the development of the embryo is influenced not only
by the cell growth, but also by the decay of cells that have just
been formed. So that the hands do not look like small paddles
later, the cells of the webbing between the fingers must die, since
only in this way do the individual fingers become flexible. Also,
the eyeballs could not completely develop without a specific
death, as the eyes are formed out of a simple indentation of the
skin into a complex sensory organ. Without the dissolution of
cell nuclei in the evolved lens, our view would be clouded in
the truest sense of the word.

Likewise, an excess of cells in the brain first emerges.
Later, through degeneration of individual cells, the cerebral
regions develop further. But the renewal does not end—quite
contrary to the assumption of neurology and brain research

in the 1990s, which held that the brain of an adult was not capable of further development. Today we know that the brain is adaptable until old age and can even compensate for the loss of a hemisphere.[1]

BUDDHISM AND SCIENCE

Modern science is more and more letting go of the notion that the human being is only a biochemical factory. The primary assumption that the brain produces the mind was obvious, since it fit well into the materialistic way of thinking and European intellectual history.[2] It was seen as a knowledge-processing machine, and consciousness was limited to something like a related supervisory function. But this left many areas unresolved, and there was the additional and fundamental problem that mind possesses characteristics that no material object manifests.

In recent years, however, brain research has increasingly broken away from this purely materialistic view and expanded the horizon of experience far beyond all neurobiological knowledge. Many observations cannot be explained through the biology of the brain in this way, and it has been increasingly proven in near-death research that lucid experiences are possible independent of the brain. Awareness cannot be limited to the brain, as the brain enables more than produces. In surveys of people with near-death experiences (NDEs), they consistently tell of feelings of calm and peace (90%), light perception (about 77%), or out-of-body experiences.[3]

Just like quantum physics, brain research today is moving well beyond the view that the only reality that exists is what can be measured or perceived through the senses. Increasingly, today's brain researchers assume that human perception is to a large extent the result of a mental construction. Thus, for example, apart from the activation of the sense organs, brain activity is almost the same whether one actually sees a sunrise at the ocean or only imagines it with eyes closed. There are also multiple indications that consciousness is not produced by the brain, but is unlimited in terms of time, space, and location.

It gets especially exciting from a Buddhist perspective where neuroscience and quantum physics meet. At this meeting point, many approaches and perspectives fill out Buddha's twenty-five-hundred-year-old teachings. While classical physics assumes an objective reality, both quantum mechanics and relativity theory break with this concept.[4] Just as in Buddhism, one proceeds here from the perspective that there is no world independent of the observer—or, as Einstein expressed it once, "Reality is merely an illusion, albeit a very persistent one."[5]

Both quantum physics and Buddhism go beyond the dualistic view, avoid the extremes of "either-or," and prefer instead the "both-and." Twelve hundred years ago, the accomplisher Saraha in northern India described it in a true-to-life way: "Anyone who thinks the world is real is as stupid as an ox. Whoever believes that it is not real is even more stupid" (because on the relative level that would go against the law of cause and effect, i.e., *karma*).

Space is seen in itself as empty of its own characteristics and yet connecting everything, containing all knowledge, and inseparable from everything. In the fall of 2004, Rupert Sheldrake asked a group of people at the University of Cambridge to guess who out of four possible and currently known participants had called them. The matches went far beyond the statistically expected 25% (from trial and error) and reached 42%.[6]

The quantum physicist Anton Zeilinger of the University of Vienna understands quantum mechanics as an information theory and has proven, for example, by experiments with "entangled particles" (photons), that the same knowledge can appear in space in different places simultaneously without any physical transmission paths.[7] Researchers sometimes have to share their Nobel prizes because they come to their conclusions at the same time and independently from one another in different countries.[8]

The fact that our universe consists ultimately of information shakes the strongly material-based sciences to their foundations and simultaneously confirms Buddha's teachings that all-encompassing space is more like a container than something that separates things—and therefore not a black hole, but something that encompasses and connects beings.[9]

If one leaves the understanding of the world that was taught up to now and follows the latest insights of quantum physics, neuroscience, and near-death research, rebirth becomes comprehensible. It is comparable to a radio; even if the device breaks, the radio programs keep on playing. If the recipient, the brain, gradually disintegrates, which is the case while dying, and can play fewer and fewer programs, the entire human being will not disappear but only his material aspect. All of his characteristics remain preserved. What one has vanishes, but what one is—the experiencer of all things—keeps on living beyond space and time. Death, like birth, is only a transition into another state of consciousness. After an intermediate state (Skt. *antarābhava*, Tib. *bardo*), where the strongest accumulated impressions come up, the experiencer of all things connects itself with a new body that matches, in a world corresponding to what the experiencer contains.

Our awareness—that which now is looking through our eyes, listening through our ears, feeling through the skin, and thinking of yesterday or tomorrow, our mind that can do all this—is in its true essence both timeless and limitless. It is like a mirror, where the images come and go but the mirror itself does not change. It is like the ocean, where the waves arise and disappear, while the ocean remains stable. That means that our awareness, from which everything arises, was never made and therefore cannot fall apart. Because the experiencer was not born, it also cannot die. Only our bodies, because they are conditioned, will die away.

The mind is that which perceives everything but is itself neither limited nor restricted by anything. It is like space. Thus, anything that happens is its free play. Whether things arise or dissolve, whether they come or go, everything shows the richness of mind. The ultimate exists at all times and everywhere. Mind constantly plays with itself, allows worlds, states of mind, inclinations, and inner experiences full of thoughts and feelings to arise in and out of itself. If nothing appears externally or internally, it shows the space of mind, its inherent possibility. If something is experienced or happens, mind shows its clarity and capacity for free play. The fact that both may be present simultaneously points to its limitlessness.

The more one understands that mind itself is indestructible, the more likely it is that expectations and fears will dissolve and one can rest freely in the moment or act. Thus one gets hooked less often in one's own imaginary world of past and future or thinks less often that one has to prove something or apologize for anything. Gradually there arises a view in which everything is exciting just because it happens and expresses the possibilities of mind. Instead of hopes and fears, one suddenly experiences space and freedom, both outside and inside, and joyfully learns how much surplus and power beings possess and are able to pass on and how much richness can develop. Whether something comes together through youth, strength and love—or dissolves through old age, sickness and death—both show the boundless play of mind, an expression of mind's unlimited and inherent possibilities.

WITHOUT BEGINNING AND END

For thousands of years human beings have speculated about the world, life, death, and what comes afterward, and countless assumptions and perspectives have been developed. The idea that there might be a beginning and an end of the world was once widespread. It can be found with the Vikings as well as in Greek thinking, or with the three major faith religions of the Middle East, in which God's people—often with difficult gods—experience them on the way to a promised land. Whereas in faith religions a personal god is the cause and final goal of their world, Buddhism and other experience-based religions—such as Hinduism and Taoism—proceed from a permanent cycle of arising and disappearing (the cycle of life).

The world is not the creation of a higher power or something objective and external, but is constantly created by perceptions and actions. That is why one can liberate oneself by developing beyond-personal insight. Instead of blaming original sin or looking for a guilty one to blame for the misfortunes of life, and instead of hoping for something otherworldly, one simply looks at the given circumstances and effects and focuses on the development of that which is, both in and after life. Accordingly, one can generally find sturdy advice for mastering one's life, death, and happy rebirth, if one turns to experience-based religions—and here especially Tibetan Buddhism.

To develop an understanding of the different states and behaviors of mind, Buddhist teachings divide the cycle of life. It consists of a constant chain of interdependent moments, but can be subdivided into intermediate states. Such intermediate states, from a certain starting point to a specific ending point, are designated by the term *bardo*. Literally translated, it means "gap" or "between." There is an infinite number of such bardos because everything is constantly changing. Up until enlightenment, one is always in transition from one state to another. Generally understood, bardo designates the intermediate state between the present life and rebirth into the following life. Only the state where the knower recognizes his own timelessness—liberation or enlightenment—is not a bardo.

In some passages of *The Tibetan Book of the Dead* one only speaks of two bardos: the one of life and the one of death. But in other passages there are four: the bardos of life, of dying, of suchness, and of becoming. Even more precise explanations distinguish two additional bardos during the intermediate state of life. This makes a total of six bardos: the one of the waking state, of dream, of meditation, of dying, of the ultimate nature, and of becoming.[10]

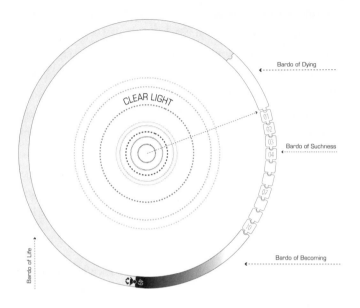

CLEAR LIGHT

Bardo of Dying

Bardo of Suchness

Bardo of Becoming

Bardo of Life

Cycle of Life

The six bardos correspond to three always recurrent states of consciousness, from birth until the moment when the process of dying has irrevocably started, and three successive intermediate states that take place between dying and the next life.

Bardo of life (Skt. *jatyantarābhava,* Tib. *rangzin bardo*): In the waking state, everybody works with the commonly experienced sensuous world through body, speech, and mind. One is aware and can think and act deliberately.

The world is experienced as being solid and logical.

During the day a common world is experienced, even though it is colored by one's own attitude. The shared part is what the range of our senses and the openness of the specific culture allow us to experience, and the personal part is the slant that one adds through one's own wishes and expectations. During that time one is able to consciously change one's life, and steer and work with one's mind (see "The Ways to Happiness" and "Rebirth").

With the help of Buddhist methods, one can best prepare for the future and therefore for all other intermediate states.

Bardo of dream (Skt. *svapanāntarābhava,* Tib. *milam bardo*): The periods of dreaming during sleep are called the second bardo within the bardo of life. This also includes states of intoxication by non-psychedelic drugs or alcohol. While dreaming, three types of experience occur during three nocturnal periods: first the impressions of the day are processed, then physical experiences can arise during deep sleep, and, just before waking up, the mind is sometimes open to events that are about to happen—whereas during undisturbed sleep visions of a more distant future are possible. The dream is experienced to be as real as the daily world, even though things happen completely freely and independently of time, place and body, are not shared with others, pertain only to the mind, and do not take place in chronological order. During deep sleep, where consciousness dwells in the middle of the body and can only be experienced by accomplishers with specific meditation practices, complete ignorance prevails.

Bardo of meditation (Skt. *samādhyantarābhava,* Tib. *samtan bardo*): An advanced Buddhist meditates regularly with the intention of recognizing his mind. During everyday activities he keeps a view as pure as possible and overlays this onto the daily, mostly habitual stream of experiences. That way one learns to react less and less to disturbing emotions, stays more conscious in each moment, and can gradually experience the timeless qualities of mind. At the end of a sitting meditation, when the daily tasks reemerge, this level will be held in the best possible way. With each meditation one not only gets to know the mind better, but the vast "both-and" awareness allows one to better command the experiences. One uses the expression "bardo of meditation" only when a direct experience of the nature of mind has actually taken place. Only then is one able to distinguish between meditation and post-meditation. Just as the shift from one realm of experience into the next (sleep/meditation) gets more and more familiar over the years, so too can one later go consciously through the process of dying, if it is physically possible, and, depending on one's ability, use it in the best way possible for the future (see "The Way to Happiness" and "Conscious Dying").

But the everyday experiences are not the only intermediate states that are lived through. If conditions for life cease, the body can no longer hold the mind. Then its energy-consciousness leaves the mind, and three more bardos appear with force.

Bardo of dying (Skt. *mumūrsāntarābhava,* Tib. *chikai bardo*): The first of these intermediate states, the bardo of dying, is the dying process itself, which is the time just before, during, and shortly after clinical death, which all beings have experienced again and again since beginningless time and will experience over and over until enlightenment (see "Conscious Dying").

Bardo of suchness (Skt. *dharmatāntarābhava,* Tib. *chönyi bardo*): During the second state, the bardo of suchness, it is possible to melt with the clear light of mind. This way one can recognize the essence of mind and become enlightened. If this moment passes without being used, approximately sixty-eight hours of unconsciousness will follow, for educated people. As soon as one awakens from this phase, Buddhists have the opportunity within the next seven days to meet their teachers and those buddha forms with which they have built up a connection through empowerment or guided meditations and to enter their power-fields of highest bliss (see "The Crucial Moment").

Bardo of becoming (Skt. *bhāvāntarābhava,* Tib. *sipai bardo*): If one has not been able to use the opportunity to reach a beyond-personal state during the previous bardo, one gets into the next intermediate state, the bardo of becoming, starting from the tenth day onward. Here the imprints in the store-consciousness, consisting of tendencies and karma, form an ever-more solid pattern, which ties oneself to a new life in the conditioned world within the following thirty-nine days (see "Rebirth").

THE TIBETAN BOOK OF THE DEAD

In the West, mainly the teachings of *The Tibetan Book of the Dead* (Tib. *bardo thödröl:* "liberation through hearing in the intermediate state") are well known. They are contained in a Buddhist scripture from the eighth century that is traced

The Six Intermediate States

bardo of life	**bardo of life**	• between conception and the beginning of the dying process • place of birth, attitude and physical dispositions are effects of karmic causes • building up and dissolving karma
	bardo of dream	• occasional consciousness during sleep • partial release from store-consciousness of those karmic impressions which one experiences as a dream • no sensory perception
	bardo of meditation	• direct experience of the nature of mind • resting in the here and now and becoming one with the lama or Buddha • resting in one's center without getting distracted by thoughts and feelings, keeping the feeling between the meditations; it is experienced beginning with the first bodhisattva-level
bardo of death	**bardo of dying**	• from the first sign of dying until mind leaves the body* (ca. 30 minutes) • loss of body, family, friends, possessions and concepts • weakening of sensory perceptions • dissolution of the elements: white (appearance), red (increase)and the blackness (attainment) occur in succession
	bardo of suchness	• from having left the body until the realization of one's own death* (ca.10 days) • opportunity to melt with the Clear Light of mind or the light forms • best chance for Phowa is at the beginning of this bardo or three days afterward
	bardo of becoming	• from the realization of one's own death until the new connection with the conditioned world in six possible realms of existence • at the beginning, continuation of the impressions of last life • impressions of all lifetimes appearing out of the store-consciousness —starting on about the 25th day* — determine the next rebirth

average times, they can vary a lot from individual to individual

Lopön Tsechu Rinpoche: "*Actually the complete concept of bardo refers to the time during which we are caught in samsara, because its foundation is our ignorance. Until we have liberated ourselves from this, that means until enlightenment, this is a bardo state, the state of ignorance until enlightenment.*"   (Rødby/Denmark, 1992) back to the founder of Tibetan Buddhism, Guru Rinpoche. It is, among others, widely recognized because of its similarity to the light phenomena of the near-death experiences that are described and explained by today's researchers. It contains teachings about the process of dying and rebirth and explains possibilities for escaping from the cycle of death and rebirth. In the three "Old" or "Red Hat" meditation schools of Tibet, it was common to read the book while living, in order to be able to recall the instructions at the time of dying and, in the intermediate state, to be able to immediately reach liberation. Also those who were deceased and now in the intermediate state were read to from the book, in order to guide them on the way to a better rebirth.

However, it is also important here not to stop thinking critically because until the Chinese conquest in 1959, which brought even more suffering, medieval conditions held sway in Tibet, with few police and marshals. The authorities— mostly landowners in Lhasa and the surrounding three major monasteries—tried to keep the population submissive by maintaining a certain level of fear in their society. This worked out pretty well with the peaceful inhabitants in the center of the country. Accordingly, they emphasized the suffering of dying and the hells afterward. If one takes current insights from research on near-death experiences into account, far better prospects arise—surely not only because of today's good painkillers and the civilized societies of Western countries. Ultimately, the impressions and images that come up in the mind after death depend on one's attitude and lifestyle.

The Buddhist teachers (Tib. *lamas*) of the three old schools of Tibet above all offer a comprehensive view of the manifold experiences and processes after death until a new rebirth. In addition, their great meditation masters, also called *accomplishers*, are the foundation of the teachings. As mind not only brings forth new experiences but also stores previous ones, these masters remember experiences from previous lives through their clear-sightedness. This explains a lot and gives unshakable certainty.

Buddha's teachings, the statements of Guru Rinpoche, experiences of Buddhist masters, and insights of others who may have practiced Buddhist meditations in past lives, confirm deep hopes: there are timeless beyond-personal levels of consciousness of highest joy, and there are methods one can learn even during life, in order at the moment of death to free mind permanently from any kind of pain, and—if one succeeds in recognizing the then emerging Clear Light as one's own nature—to realize even enlightenment itself. These practices, encompassing body, speech and mind, are called *Phowa* in Tibetan, and the easiest and most usable for everyone is described in the chapter called "Conscious Dying." This meditation weakens mortal fears already during life and automatically brings those who have learned it into so-called pure (i.e. liberated and exceedingly joyful) levels of consciousness from which there is no falling back.

Anyone who wishes to develop all abilities and qualities in these realms, which are inherent in mind, should decide at an early stage to use the dying process for this purpose. At no other time do the conditions for giant leaps of development come together as beneficially as here: when all sensory impressions fall away, habits dissolve, and all energies are concentrated, then the path opens onto a vast field of development. Depending on one's insight and courage, one will recognize one's mind more and more deeply as timeless truth, self-arisen joy, and active love.

THE WAYS TO HAPPINESS

Even if one had the same good conditions that Buddha had twenty-five hundred years ago—a kingdom, friends, lovers, servants, education, sports, health and a joyful mind—one would still have to realize one day that impermanence does not stop at one's own front door and that all outer joys continually die away. Even if with good luck one manages not to get sick, one would certainly not get around old age and death. When, at the age of twenty-nine, Buddha met sickness, old age and death, he spent one of the following long nights pondering, until he recognized that this painful process of life is inevitable. The next morning he looked into the eyes of an accomplisher and understood: there is a timeless experiencer on which one can rely—beyond the experiences, always and everywhere. To realize this awareness for the benefit of all seemed to him the most meaningful goal ever, and so he set out to do just that.

THE FOUR NOBLE TRUTHS

After his enlightenment at the age of thirty-five, Buddha, "the Awakened One," started his forty-five-year-long teaching with four key statements:

"There is suffering." This statement is not as pessimistic as clueless people experience it at first sight and as it is still understood in many universities today. Rather, upon a closer look, it points to the unlimited richness that is inherent in mind. Compared to the timeless bliss that is the ultimate nature of everybody, each conditioned experience remains more or less full of suffering, and even the most beautiful moments in life manifest only fragmentary insights of this bliss. Buddha distinguished three types of suffering. The "suffering of suffering" is experienced when everything breaks down and one feels neither outer nor inner support, as with heavy losses, separation, invincible pain, or when dying without lasting values. The "suffering of impermanence" describes that one cannot hold on to anything and that all happiness, all that is beautiful and pleasant, will in the end dissolve between one's fingers. The "suffering of ignorance" finally indicates not being enlightened, and therefore being unable to understand "the way things are."[11] While keeping busy with the first two unsubtle forms of suffering, one rarely experiences the much more subtle third one. But this one is the root cause of all suffering and dissolves only with full enlightenment.

"Suffering has a cause." All beings look for happiness and want to avoid suffering, but they often reap the opposite. Human beings do control the outside world through their knowledge, but the inner world in most people does what it wants and, if it includes body and speech, causes the behavior that leads to suffering. Since something ultimately evil would always destroy itself, according to the law of cause and effect, the only logical explanation that remains for suffering is one's own stupidity. The unenlightened mind is like an eye that perceives the outer phenomena very well but is not able to see itself. It is precisely this basic ignorance that causes all misery. Although anything personal—be it body, mind or feelings—cannot demonstrate any lasting and real existence because it is constantly changing, mind experiences itself through the senses as an "I" that is separated from totality, due to the above-mentioned ignorance. This in turn makes the outer world that is experienced through the senses a "you"—something separated from oneself. Holding on to this duality and understanding body, speech and mind as "I" prevents all ultimate happiness. Going after ever-growing needs always leads to disappointment. As long as the false illusion of an "I" that is real and separated from the totality survives, everyone is vulnerable. Then one takes all experiences as personal, looks at the world from a very narrow angle, and makes mistakes.

The results of this error are desire for what seems to be missing and aversion to what keeps one away from the supposed happiness. The unpleasant states of confusion, desire and aversion lead to ugly subsequent emotions: silly pride which, in putting others down, harms one's own attitude to life in the long run, as well as avarice, envy and hatred. Their countless combinations (Buddha speaks of 84,000 possible ones) cause further disturbing emotions, mental veils, and confusions. They are the cause of all clumsy and difficult actions, words, and thoughts.

If one does not get an overview of the processes mentioned above and continues to act on the basis of one's feelings, in spite of their clearly visible volatility, one is already in the difficult cycle of cause and effect. Thus, one constantly experiences the effects of former actions without being aware that they have been self-induced, and, therefore, one again puts shortsighted, harmful, or clumsy actions into the world. The cycles of limitation and suffering that inevitably arise as a result have an effect permanently and everywhere and, until the complete dissolution of this basic misconception, they influence the entire life and reach beyond death.

"There is an end of suffering." Buddha's third statement is heart-warming: here he did not speak of things that he had from hearsay or that had happened elsewhere, but rather verified the joyful statement with his own example.

What is explained so humbly is actually omniscience and continuous highest bliss, nothing else but enlightenment. There is an experience for which it is worth striving, a timeless, real refuge that already dwells in everyone and that one has only to discover. This state is fearless space, and the experience of it is lasting highest joy. With that, every word and every action is accompanied by far-sighted wisdom and active love. Without the separation of an "I" here and a "you" somewhere else, mind shines like a sun that radiates effortlessly on its own. Buddha showed this ultimate state continuously to the very end of his life, combining insight and compassion in word and action.

"There is a way to the end of suffering." With this fourth statement he made everything tangible. In his teaching style it became apparent that in the long run he wanted colleagues rather than devout followers. Instead of dogmatically prescribing how or what to think or believe, he taught his students to question everything critically and to recognize the true coherences of life for themselves. As he died, his last words were: "I can leave this place happily. Everything that can benefit you I have already given." Given that such statements could have easily led to a lack of independence, he added: "Now don't believe a single word just because a Buddha said it but examine everything yourself. Be your own Clear Light." This was an explicit demand to his students not to reach for dogmas but to check everything through one's own experience.

The task that he gave was to take over responsibility for oneself, and he taught this on various levels, depending on the difference in his students' orientation. To those who primarily want to dissolve their own suffering, he gave the teachings of Southern Buddhism, also called Theravada or Foundational Vehicle. Those who mainly want to benefit others out of compassion and with insight, he enriched with the methods of Northern Buddhism, known as Mahayana or Great Way. Finally he held the shining mirror of their own buddha nature up to the students who dare to make the big leap and want to act like a buddha until they become one, and these are the views and practices of Vajrayana or Diamond Way.

After Buddha's death, his students spent months together collecting his teachings, and several of them had a crystal clear memory. In this way came to be the 108 (sometimes 103 or 106) books and eighty-four thousand teachings of the Kanjur, the (Tibetan) collection of his teachings. It was later expanded by the Tenjur, which are subsequent explanations by Indian masters. It comprises 254 similarly thick volumes.

In essence, Buddha's path consists of three pillars: knowledge, which should be questioned; meditation, where what is recognized as valid and useful slides from the head into the heart and enriches one; and, a way of behaving that enables the practitioner to experience the effect of the teachings and to secure them effectively.

Three Kinds of Suffering	
❶	**The suffering of ignorance** The all-pervading suffering, which dominates as long as one is not enlightened.
❷	**The suffering of change** Each conditioned happiness brings about suffering in the end; that means if fortunate conditions fall away, suffering begins.
❸	**The suffering of suffering** This suffering is very noticeable. It appears in all realms of existence.

THE FOUR BASIC THOUGHTS

From a Buddhist perspective happiness and joy do not depend on outer conditions, which change constantly, but on the experiencer of all phenomena—mind itself. Therefore, one looks for completion by turning one's attention inward. Mind, in its essence, is a shining mirror whose radiance, however, is clouded by veils from former experiences and from the more or less human cultural background into which one was born with one's karma. What appears in it—its images—is impermanent and ultimately not real. Only the mirror itself lasts. So it makes sense to focus on the experiencer itself and not the prancing and fast-moving phenomena within it.

Buddha's key method for this purpose is meditation (Skt. *bhavana* or *sadhana*, Tib. *gom*). Only through directly working with mind does one find a level of satisfaction in which the outer world and possessions benefit one and produce space for the development of real and lasting values. For this, the observation of mind, as well as the life stories

of realized masters and of Buddha himself, give direction
to one's own path of development. By their timelessness
they show how they can master their own lives, while at
the same time, endowed with fearlessness, joy and love,
they think of others and help them at all times. For some
people such examples are enough for them to open up to the
Buddhist methods and to use the meditations that they have
learned. Others are shaken by losses since, unfortunately,
most people only notice the happy moments when they
have already disappeared. Just as the values of youth and
health are only recognized through old age and sickness, so
is life sadly often appreciated only when death is imminent.
To successfully discover mind with joy and endurance, one
needs a goal-orientation and a trove of insights that opens
one up for the here and now.

Therefore, all work with mind starts with four basic
observations. They provide direction and grant goal and
meaning to each meditation from the beginning:

The first basic thought focuses on the precious opportunity to use one's own life for development using Buddhist
methods. If one has come into contact with Buddha's teachings, one has the very rare opportunity to recognize the experiencing, timeless mind through all-encompassing wisdom
and to come to know boundless happiness. It is important
to understand how precious this is, because very few people
meet Buddhist teachings and even fewer are able to use
them. The traditional teachings refer to eight freedoms and
ten endowments (i.e. conditions that must come together
for this purpose):

Eight Freedoms

One was not reborn:

1	... in a hell realm
2	... in a ghost realm
3	... in an animal realm
4	... in a god realm
5	... in a country without Buddhist teachings
6	... with people who have wrong views and do not recognize that beneficial actions are the precondition for a fortunate rebirth and liberation
7	... in a world where there are neither fully enlightened beings nor teachings
8	... with serious mental disabilities

Ten Fortunate Conditions

Five conditions that depend on us:

1	to be a human being
2	to be born in a more developed country
3	to be in control of one's senses
4	to not be burdened with extremely negative actions
5	to have trust in the appropriate methods

Five conditions that depend on others:

6	A fully awakened one has appeared in this world.
7	He has taught the noble teachings.
8	His teachings have been preserved.
9	The preserved teachings are practiced.
10	There are beings who lovingly care for others.

If one misses the infinitely precious opportunity to recognize the nature of one's mind and through this experience the highest completion, it is uncertain how many lives without this ultimate view will follow before such fortunate conditions will appear again. Birth, old age, sickness and death are full of suffering with every rebirth. Even the most beautiful conditioned experiences pale beside the permanent joy of realization.

The second basic thought consists of bringing into view the impermanence of everything composite. Whether one is aware of it or not, nothing will last. Everything comes and goes—even our body—and one does not know when one will lose it. To avoid wasting time, Buddha advises us to observe closely the changing seasons, the flow of the days and moments, and to develop a general awareness of impermanence.

This teaching provides a special glint of hope if sometimes everything is upside down: the wife runs away with the mailman, the uninsured house burns down, or the police bring the children back home yet again. Even these circumstances are temporary! Nothing is lasting. Fortunately, it is the same with the difficult inner states. They are in constant motion and therefore can be influenced. The less attention one pays to them, the quicker they will dissolve again.

Whoever understands the elusiveness of all appearances will make something of his or her life. For, as soon as one is aware of the rare and exceedingly precious situation that is given in today's Western societies with regard to freedom and education, one will not uselessly waste one's time but will hopefully use it for the development of the highest possible meaningful qualities.

The third basic thought deals with cause and effect. The different life situations and feelings that we experience do not happen accidentally but are determined by our attitude and our own actions. From the very moment when consciousness connects with the egg and the sperm, everyone already expresses impressions from past lives. These form the basis for the present life: the liberties or limitations of one's cultural sphere; the behavior of parents and one's body; and conditions that in turn influence health, talent and inclinations. Accordingly, already today one can consciously steer the direction of future lives and, by skillful thoughts, words and actions, often also change the current circumstances that are maturing in this moment. If one chooses to be kind, one will be able to spend one's time more and more often in good company and if one gives no additional power to fears, mind becomes courageous and can relax. If one helps the sick and dying, one's friends will surely also gather around when one needs it.

One's own past is responsible for how well one is doing today. As long as one does not consciously shape the stream of impressions and actions, then previous thoughts, words, and actions will continue to determine how future living conditions will be molded. One will also be chased neither by a revengeful god nor by a so-called fate but can create one's own life. What freedom!

If one understands that the compelling qualities and abilities of all enlightened beings are also the results of their past actions, sowing the proper causes for the good of all beings is immediately recognized as a skillful means for one's own life. Buddha, who treated his students as adults, summarized in a practical manner both useful and harmful behavior into ten contrasting points, which should be understood as a wise friend's advice and not as commandments. They form the cornerstones of a good and free development of body, speech, and mind. Here, in the words of Gampopa, founder of the *Kagyü* monastic lineages in the twelfth century, is a short list of behaviors that will bring happiness or suffering for beings in the future:

Actions and Their Effects

	meaningful actions		harmful actions	
	action	*effect*	*action*	*effect*
Body	protecting life	healthy, long life *(good conditions for life)*	killing	short life full of sickness *(difficult conditions for life)*
	generosity	richness, the feeling of always having enough	stealing/ deceiving	poverty; loss; birth in a country with a lot of frost and hail
	causing sexual joy	harmony, kindness	causing sexual harm	hostile partner; birth in a desert or a very dusty region
Speech	telling the truth	hearing the truth, being respected	lying/ building up false trust	slander; unpleasant bad breath
	creating harmony	bringing people together and having many friends	separating people/ slandering	being separated from friends; birth in hilly, jagged regions
	speaking calmly and trustworthily	hearing pleasant things about oneself	talking roughly	hearing unpleasant things about oneself; birth in an arid, hot country with people who do lots of negative things
	meaningful speech	speech bringing changes	meaningless gossip	things said are disregarded; birth in a region where the seasons get mixed up
Mind	being modest and content	balanced state of mind, free of expectations	greed	disappointment; insatiability; birth in a country with bad harvests
	being benevolent	trust in others	ill will	fear; aversion; birth in a rough region with bitter fruits of bad quality
	developing the right view	having the ability to understand the Buddhist teachings	wrong views	stupidity; birth in a region where there are no fruits; degenerate philosophy

According to the classical teachings of Gampopa[12]

Buddha's recommendations make it easier to do the right thing. Good results are no longer dependent on someone else or a higher being who sees or rewards the good action, but they appear of their own accord. Also, it is natural to resist the many little odd temptations to bend the truth for one's own benefit or not to pay for the bus ticket, taxes, or a lecture. The daily understanding of cause and effect brings certainty to the actions. Any doubt whether something is meaningful or has an effect, dissolves with it.

The fourth basic thought emphasizes the attitude to mentally develop oneself for the good of all. The observation that one can do only a little for others as long as one is confused or suffering opens one up to Buddha's life, teachings, and methods. Without having gained an overview through this observation, one easily sits in the nettles instead of the flowers and even well-intended thoughts, words and actions can, through personal entanglements and confusion, unintentionally lead to more suffering than joy. In such moments one wistfully wishes for wise solutions. Here, Buddha's advice is a rich treasure and, combined with meditation, is in the end the only way to an unshakable beyond-personal experience. Merely thinking high-mindedly about the purpose of life and death doesn't bring progress. Enlightenment is not only timeless but also more beautiful, truer, and more indestructible than anything separable or conditioned. There is no greater happiness than the full development of mind!

FINDING LASTING HAPPINESS

To be able to change one's behavior and make it last, it is

necessary to recognize the causes of the common actions already
on the way and to consciously allow a lot of space between the
experiencer and the experiences. With every disturbing influence
one tries to extend the span between stimulus and action and
to understand that right now one is creating one's future. In
this way, one learns in everyday life that, when encountering
difficult people, it is better to chew a dozen sticks of gum at
the same time than to answer with something hurtful or to
consciously sit on one's hands rather than sending a fellow
human to the hospital. If one recognizes that unpleasant people
are always trapped in their disturbing emotions and have very
little freedom of choice, it is easy to see them as patients and to
develop compassion for them.

The intelligent person recognizes cause and effect as well
as the changeability and unreality of all things and therefore
tries consciously to do each possible good action—even the
smallest—with a clear overview and compassion and to avoid
everything harmful. Actually, small direct causes very often
bring about large effects.

Generally speaking, the essence of all Buddhist development
is simply purifying disturbing emotions and removing stiff ideas.
The buddha nature is already inherent in us! It is like climbing
a tower: useful actions for the good of all bring advantage in
vertical height and view. When entanglements and unpleasant
impressions slowly dissolve, vastness and clarity of mind gradually emerge. Meaningful thinking, speaking, and acting lead to
pleasant and flowing feedback experiences with the surrounding
world and one's own store-consciousness. And last, but not least:
good habits simply feel pleasant.

To have perspective on mind, to pacify and hold it, which

forms the basis for precise and powerful work with mind, some Buddhist schools use deeply effective perceptual images, while others prefer to work without forms. The most widely known is the practice of counting the breath and/or feeling the stream of air at the tip of the nose. The goal here is to turn the mind to itself step by step, but at the same time, not to let it get unclear, but rather to bring forth its innate ability—in Buddhist terms called clarity. This is similar to what happens with muddy water where, after being at rest for some time, its mud settles and it gets clear. Generally this creates more distance from one's own emotions. In this way one increasingly gets to choose to take on many roles in the comedies of life and stay clear of its tragedies. Protection from getting trapped by the experiences is achieved because of increased inner awareness, which slowly but surely gives one the freedom to act wisely for the good of all. The two above-mentioned stages of pacifying the mind and insight (called *shinay* and *lhaktong* in Tibetan or *shamata* and *vipashyana* in Sanskrit) can be found in all Buddhist meditations. In Diamond Way one uses buddha forms instead of the formless breathing. First one imagines them in detail (building-up phase; Tib. *kyerim*), then uses their mantras, and then melts with them at the end (melting phase; Tib. *dzogrim*). As different and multi-layered as the methods may appear at first sight, one always aligns oneself with the desired goal, the wished-for state or Buddha, and then realizes it. An example of a practice that can be used by everybody without instructions, that calms the mind and gives distance to emotions, is the meditation on the breath.[13]

The peace of mind and power reached through the state

of absorption not only help one to endure inevitable difficulties in life such as sickness, suffering or loss more easily, but they also give the necessary equanimity and fearlessness for the last moments of life. Since most people have very little access to their situation and state of mind, especially while dying—not to mention any influence on it—they easily become discomfited by their constantly changing emotions. If, over the years, the habit has developed to watch one's mind in the state of absorption and to control it more and more, this is particularly helpful on the deathbed. The hard-pressed mind finds support in the familiar and trained methods and can more easily compose itself.

REFUGE

How can trust in mind be developed in such a way that, both in life and death, every experience is lived as enriching and meaningful?

One starts with the profound focus on three values that one can really trust. All Buddhists open up to this so-called refuge, in order to enter the way of development. These three values are:

Buddha (Tib. *sangye*), who embodies the perfect realization of mind on all levels and shows by his example that, as a human being, one can enlighten oneself and, in this manner, experience and express fearless wisdom, self-arisen joy, and active love. This buddha nature is inherent in everybody, even if one is not aware of it.

The teachings, the way to enlightenment (Skt. *dharma*, Tib. *chö*), consisting of Buddha's eighty-four thousand teachings. They make it possible for everybody to reach their goal with the wished-for speed and offer assistance, in any situation, from an enlightened view.

The friends on the way (Skt. *sangha,* Tib. *gendün*). They are the famous, as well as the many unnoticed, bodhisattvas, with whose help one can develop.

Together they are called the "Three Jewels" or "Rare" and "Precious" ones (Skt. *tri ratna,* Tib. *könchog sum*).

If one aims for the ultimate experience of mind, enlightenment, one has to utilize all levels of its totality for one's development. In addition to the Three Jewels, the Diamond Way student is given the gift of the Three Roots (Skt. *trimūla,* Tib. *tsa sum*). They are sources of tremendous growth and exciting tools for developing oneself quickly and powerfully into the state of highest joy.

The first and most important root is the teacher (Skt. *guru,* Tib. *lama*), who embodies the transmission lineage and overlooks the changing moods and trips of the students. Thanks to his honesty and experience, the blessing of the buddhas is conveyed in its purity and clarity. Through his power-field and the transmission of his lineage, the lama bestows blessing, a good, warm feeling of trust that life has meaning and can be made important for many.

Secondly, he gives refuge in the buddha forms (Skt. *deva,* Tib. *yidam*), the attractive, athletic forms of light and energy, often in union, to which Tibetan Buddhism owes much of its renown worldwide. They connect the mind of the practitioner with his buddha nature, and the melting and becoming one with them gives special abilities.

Finally, the exceedingly powerful protectors (Skt.

dharmapala, Tib. *chökyong* or *gönpo*) are the third root. Because of their powerful forms, surrounded by flames and carrying weapons, they are often mistakenly considered to be hostile. They have a wisdom eye in the forehead, protect both the teachings and the students, and awaken massive activity.[14]

Because the buddha forms express common states of consciousness on an enlightened level, they are an enormous help and a great mirror for our mind—whether peace-giving, enriching, fascinating, or powerfully protecting.

The Three Jewels and Three Roots express the enlightenment that is inherent in every being. They show goal, path, and friends on the way and bring blessing, inspiration, and protection. They reflect our timeless nature. The familiar feeling that many experience when they meet them arises because these qualities are already ours, and have been since beginningless time.

Refuge	
One turns to lasting values. *One takes refuge in:*	• **Buddha**—the goal
	• the **Dharma** (Buddha's teachings)—the way
	• the **Sangha**—the bodhisattvas, the friends on the way
	and additionally in Diamond Way: • the **Lama**—the lama who today represents the 17th Karmapa Thaye Dorje. The lama embodies the Three Jewels of enlightenment—Buddha, his teachings and the liberated sangha—as well as the Three Roots of blessing, realization and protection.

Not only is refuge useful as a direction for daily development, it can also be very helpful, in unexpected or dramatic experiences in life, to remember the lama or Buddha since he contains the entire power-field of the refuge. To think of the lama in moments of disturbance gives inner certainty, and each blessing that one's own karma allows grows stronger. Above all, there is no better refuge in death than a spiritual friend or teacher whom one trusts.

WAYS AND METHODS IN DIAMOND WAY

All Buddhist paths have the following in common: refuge in the Three Jewels, the understanding of cause and effect, and the Four Noble Truths. The goal of the foundational path is to dissolve the ego-attachment, which is liberation, whereby the end of all future rebirths with their suffering through birth, old age, sickness, and death is achieved. Even more far-reaching, however, is the refuge in connection with the Bodhisattva Promise, including the all-encompassing wish to develop for the good of all beings and to be reborn as long as one can be beneficial to others. The emphasis on this Great Way is the accumulation of compassion and wisdom, which is achieved through the Six Liberating Actions (see "Terminal Care"). The goal here is enlightenment for the good of all beings. If one is able to adjust one's values from being conditioned and impermanent to being ultimate and time-less—and get enthusiastic about forms of light and energy and experience the world as being pure and dreamlike—the methods of the Diamond Way are the right ones. Depending on one's own personal approach, one can use formed and formless practices in three possible ways: the Way of Trust, the Way of Methods, and the Way of Insight.

Three Ways in Diamond Way		
Common Goal Realization and highest view of the Great Seal		
Way of Methods	Way of Trust	Way of Insight
Work with inner energies (Six Teachings of Naropa, including *Phowa*) Meditation on forms of light and energy (Tib. *yidam*)	Becoming one with the lama (Tib. *lami naljor*, Skt. *guru yoga*)	Pacifying of mind (Tib. *shinay*, Skt. *shamata*) Clear seeing (Tib. *lhaktong*, skt. *vipashyana*)
The paths support and complement one another.		
Common Beginning Four Basic Thoughts, refuge, bodhisattva attitude and Foundational Practices		

The Three Ways in Diamond Way

These three ways have methods that can also be used in the process of dying and after death. They will be mentioned repeatedly as examples in the following chapters. One core theme is meditation. With the right attitude, it leads to good behavior; one gets more relaxed, gains surplus for oneself as well as for others, and is able to understand one's fellow humans better in the long run. This leads to auspicious imprints in mind. One becomes more open and joyful, sees the feelings and wishes as they come and go in mind, and, therefore, over time, needs less from the outside.

The Way of Trust

The quickest access to enlightenment is a close connection to one's own teacher. Here, very many qualities of mind mature and "inspired empathy" develops. The ability for fascination and the deep trust in the teacher as an expression of one's inherent possibilities are very skillful means to dissolve one's own limitations and habits. This way is called *guru yoga* in Sanskrit or *lami naljor* in Tibetan. It has always been the special power of the Kagyü lineage and remains still today the main pillar of the Diamond Way centers that have come into existence in the West since 1971. The meditations on the transmission and one's own teacher, in the form of the Karmapas, help more students to open up to their inherent potential than any other practice.

Devotion, however, must necessarily be connected to human maturity and the lama must be seen as a mirror of one's own qualities. Confidence in the teacher must not lead to dependency, lack of humor, or compulsive imitation. Scandals that sometimes appear in various monasteries and sects illustrate how harmful blind imitation is. Instead, the teacher should skillfully make the fearless space beyond birth and death—a space that he has himself won—accessible to the student, and, in this way, make the student independent. In the experiences that always reflect the freedom of this space, one finds the perfect qualities that have always been inherent in everybody's mind. Many yogis, among them also the great 16th Karmapa and the famous Dilgo Khyentse Rinpoche, praise the guru yoga as an independent and highly effective way. If one chooses this path of becoming one, at the end of one's life one melts into the conscious space of the teacher and simply exhales.

The Way of Insight

The Way of Insight came to Tibet with Marpa around the year 1050. It was a gift from his second main teacher Maitripa, about whom little has been known until now. This way uses both conceptual explanations as well as holistic methods such as conscious breathing to keep the mind in one place and to calm it down. In the case of Marpa's root lama, Naropa, powerful experiences shake up every notion, until direct insight arises and the unity of the experiencer, the experienced, and the experience becomes timeless. Several lamas offer meditations without tools, before or immediately after refuge, where one "merely" looks at mind—a practice that I find questionable.

Although the goal of the meditation can be easily described, a formless way requires, above all, extensive teachings on the behavior of mind as well as proper support from the teacher and the Buddhist group, along with a targeted build-up of good impressions. Most importantly, the mind should stay calm only as long as it is completely aware at the same time. Otherwise, the mental result can easily become a judgmental running after thoughts or a dull mental block, instead of the radiance of a sparkling diamond. For this reason, in Tibet these teachings were given only after thorough preparation. In fact, the real calming and holding of mind without tools and aids is much more difficult than learning yard-long mantras and the attributes of thousand-armed buddha forms.

The particular advantage of Maitripa's way is its wide applicability. With enough support and a friendly exchange with the surrounding world, his practices can be fluently integrated into daily life, even with moderate devotion and without retreats.

The Way of Methods

Nine hundred and fifty years ago the hero Marpa also brought the Way of Methods from India to Tibet over the Himalayan Mountains. Today the whole world knows the various buddha forms that are used here as a meditation support. As different as they appear, they show—after explanation and transmission from an experienced teacher—the numerous abilities and qualities of mind in its pure form. Marpa had received the teachings from his main teacher, the accomplisher Naropa, whose life story still impresses people today. This path, also called "The Six Teachings of Naropa," opens the internal energy-channels and energy-wheels of the body through inner images and conscious deep breathing.

Such methods can only be used after having finished the Foundational Practices and years of experience meditating on a buddha form.[15] Nowadays, some of these Six Teachings of Naropa are hardly usable for people who are involved in life, and their secret transmission would not have survived without the brave women and men who stayed in retreat for months and even years—something that was essential and that the Tibetan form of economy made possible.

Basically, one should not practice secret teachings—including those from other schools—without permission, instruction, and a protected framework. After unsuccessful attempts, this can lead to wounded pride and make it difficult to get access to all other transmissions in future lives.

Given a capable teacher with full transmission, the Phowa, the final practice of the Six Teachings of Naropa, is one exception for today's world. It is the most meaningful way to prepare for the moment of death and has proven to be learnable within a few days without years of preparation.

On the Great Way one stabilizes mind through strong good wishes for all beings or rests in the understanding and, better still, the experience of the mutual conditionality of all phenomena and their emptiness of having a nature of their own. Through the building-up phase in Diamond Way meditations and with the help of empowerment or guided meditation, a relaxed but, at the same time, alert and clear state arises through openness and trust. Here, calling to mind the buddha forms of light and energy, which reflect its inherent abilities, mind experiences its qualities on an enlightened level. It lives through them as real and often overwhelming because the experience of mind itself outshines all impressions that come and go in it.

Meditation used during the process of dying means not being swept away by one's agitated mind. Thus one repeatedly is able to stay on top of things, even in what is perhaps the most exciting time of one's life and, on this basis, can receive good influences and use all means in order to come through death in the best way possible. Therefore, it is very worthwhile to develop a habit of mind practices early on—practiced and mastered, of course. This provides the necessary support for the dying throughout the whole dying process, lets one endure pain better, and dissolves fears and attachments.

The increasing experience of experiencer's insight of compassion and wisdom—and, in the guru yoga practice, the joy and thankfulness when melting with the enlightened one in front of you—develops a deep awareness while dissolving all forms into the timeless, boundless, all perceiving space. This immediate and ultimately boundless insight is called *vipashyana* (Skt.) or *lhaktong* (Tib.). If one has realized this advanced practice, one looks into the Clear Light during death and feels at home (see "The Crucial Moment").

PREPARATION FOR DEATH

Every day and everywhere one has the experience that everything composite is impermanent. What was alive a moment ago is now perhaps already dead, and what appears today may already disappear tomorrow. Although used-up cells hopefully will renew themselves for a long time, everybody is dying a bit all the time. The loss of loved ones, parents, siblings, close friends or one's own health, as well as big outer changes from natural disasters or in the life of the economy, all always point to impermanence. Life certainly has an end but the intellect does not want to know anything about it and hopes for continuity, for immortality. Although it is obvious that every being will die one day, many people, who otherwise can comprehend almost everything, skillfully avoid facing this fact—often to the very end of life. The longing for certainty and immortality is a very strong human tendency and, especially in cultures that block death out, pressure to cling to life increases. However, if one understands that the only thing that remains timeless is the richness of one's own buddha nature, one can relax even with regard to death.

What the one who is dying has to remember is what Milarepa, the great accomplisher of Tibet nine hundred years ago, was singing of again and again. With true-to-life examples, mostly from nature in its direct environment in the Himalayas, he gave his students an understanding of the impermanence of all phenomena. He showed the changeable nature of the outer world as well as the unreliable and unsatisfactory nature all conditioned states of mind. He repeatedly referred his students to the only real constant: the fully developed mind.

The great female accomplisher Manibhadra recognized this when she went to fetch water from a creek with a clay pot.[16] A root tripped her; the pot slipped from her hands and broke. In that very moment she experienced directly the unity of form and space, inside and outside, as inseparable. Of course, this was only possible because for years her mind had been trained by blessing, teaching, and the state of absorption. If one is successful in this process on the way to enlightenment, disentanglement from an "I" or a "self" is the first step. With this insight all disturbing emotions fall away, and one is liberated. If one can also dissolve the persistence of stiff ideas, enlightenment itself manifests as a self-arisen and effortless development of body, speech and mind. Just as what is in the jar, when broken, becomes one with the surroundings, death offers the opportunity to recognize the basic truth of all existence through non-discriminating one-pointedness. Like space, the essence of mind is unaffected by transition and death.

HAVING THE END IN MIND IN THE HERE AND NOW

Since every moment can be the last one, one should use one's time meaningfully in any case. Neither a relaxed, pleasant life with a thirty-five-hour work week nor the run after money, a lottery win, a fulfilling lover or a house are permanently satisfying. Behind all experiences, no matter how unique they are, there always hides the pain that ultimately nothing is lasting. So, how is one able to give one's best in life and at the same time prepare for dying? How does one manage to look death straight in the eye without fear or other limiting emotions?

People can learn from almost any life situation. A constant guideline should be the law of cause and effect: actions, words, and thoughts create the future. All the impressions that are sent into the world as well as one's own store-consciousness will ripen sooner or later and lead to experiences with the same emotional content. Thus, the intelligent person gets rid of his legacies whenever they appear and stores up auspicious impressions. There are always opportunities to support others with body, speech and mind and to clear up what is smoldering and difficult within oneself. If one helps others to find timeless values, it creates good connections for this and all future lives.

To bring happiness to others is more important than many think. Those who believe that, considering today's usual competition, "winning at all costs" leads to lasting success should know that people are not seeing one another for the first or the last time. An honest and upright exchange with others, in which hopefully everyone experiences advantage, is therefore the best way to long-term success for all involved. On the other hand, a blind or toothless horse that was sold as if in perfect condition in an earlier life will, if not purified by a good lifestyle, later lead to a bad meeting in this life.

People meet one another again if there was already a relationship in earlier lives and, as one notices in the press every day, connections can be many-faceted. In order that current troublemakers do not appear again in future lives, one can habitually do something good for them today, with the wish that they become very happy, as far away as possible.

Another useful action is to constantly forgive all unpleasant people. Then one doesn't have to carry them along as excess baggage through a life that is otherwise hopefully exciting. The precious freedom of being able to forgive dissolves the shared bad karma, and difficult beings will come back as friends or not appear again in a future life. On the other hand, if we keep the grudge, we do not get rid of them and the annoying sandbox games do not end. Even on our deathbed we can still excuse ourselves for our own stupid behavior and express our gratitude toward others. This not only redeems us but also the friends who are involved.

> In the mid 1980s I was invited to a beautiful home near Los Angeles where an elderly, deeply embittered woman lived and could not die despite all signs of weakness. Her husband had transferred AIDS to her. It was the time before the new life-prolonging drugs. She was already sitting in a wheelchair and the husband—still healthy—lurked around like a shadow. After I had talked with her and blessed her, she understood that he was as unhappy as she was and was then, deeply relieved, able to forgive him.

Until recently, this was more Buddhist than psychological wisdom, but the latest research on positive psychology confirms that people who generously forgive others and wish them everything good, feel better, despite the suffering that the others have caused.[17] Forgiveness is simply less prickly than revenge and anger.

While dying, all the accumulated impressions of the past life condense and thus determine the inner experiences. Therefore one chooses during one's lifetime whether one will die in a relaxed and fearless way.

The mastery of mind gained in life and the understanding of the ultimate reality also determine whether one will be able to work with mind during dying and to comprehend the experience of death. One does not realize mind's maturity through the kind of emotions that one has at this moment, but through the distance one has from them. In the process of dying, the untrained mind usually wavers back and forth; it experiences clarity and confusion in turns, and can recall things understood only sketchily. If the sensory impressions cannot give any support to mind anymore, one's only protection are one's own good actions or those that are done in one's name, along with the good wishes of the bereaved.

If one already gives one's best in life and tries to be aware as much as possible, hope and fear at the moment of death will have little space and one will hardly feel any regret. Instead, one can release oneself fully into the process, because nothing else matters.

To die without fear and to use death as a springboard into the all-liberating space, one must start early—that means now. What is called for is to observe mind, get to know it, develop confidence in it, and build up useful habits as soon as possible. Though it is true in this context that Buddhist knowledge is a great help and gives a broad overview, only regular meditation and keeping the view in everyday life dissolve unwanted habits and reduce the influence of disturbing emotions, such as stupidity, anger, jealousy, attachment, avarice and pride.

No matter in which form one acquires the wisdom—be it through the example of the teacher, through books, or through lectures—without regular application of the teachings and meditation, that means without experience, little will change. Untapped knowledge is like a map: it can point out the way and grant an overview, but it does not go the way. Thus the understanding of the path is only the first step.

Amid the pleasures and distractions of today's life, one needs practice and honesty with oneself in order to recognize and give up outer and inner tendencies that will bring harm, and instead to incorporate useful ones. Because long-held internalized views and attitudes appear especially powerful in death, the daily practice should include body, speech and mind, so that the teachings slide from the head to the heart as fast as possible. It is certain and a real gift that the Buddhist methods will help in both this life and afterward.

ACCEPTING AND LETTING GO

Death has countless causes. Either the life span has simply run out or sudden circumstances lead to death. With the former, one can only mitigate the experiences because death itself is inevitable. But if life is unexpectedly threatened apparently out of nowhere, sometimes medicine, meditation, and long-life empowerments or wishes may still help to extend one's life.

In general, diseases develop because of an imbalance of energies in the body or a prevalence of the disturbing emotions of attachment, anger and confusion. Such harmful impressions can cause fear, discomfort, or even passing away. It does not matter if disease and, ultimately, death are caused by an imbalance in the body or through states of mind. The cause of any suffering—seen from a Buddhist perspective—is always the clinging to the wrong idea of a lasting ego.

How does one know that one will die and what one will experience in the process?

When relatives whom one hasn't seen for a long time come to visit, make special efforts on one's behalf, and wish that one signs papers, or the friends look unhappy and the enemies happy, or the doctor wants his payment at once, then the others might know more of one's state of health than oneself. In this case, it would be wise to adjust to possible death.

A sign of approaching death is an intense change of character, often observed even in animals, because the usual energy streams change in the body. Someone who was previously known for his kindness and generosity can suddenly become agitated, get angry and cling to everything, whereas difficult people can become remarkably nice.

The news of one's imminent death rarely leaves anyone untouched. In most cases it unleashes a whole flood of emotions and conflicting thoughts: beginning with refusing to believe, disappointment, anger, and envy for all who do not have to suffer or can live on, and going all the way to loneliness, apathy, or the strong wish to live longer since so much seems unfinished.

Especially when the death is accompanied by physical decline, one can discern different types of people. There are some who stubbornly suppress what is happening to them, to the last breath. They simply refuse to face the facts. On the other hand, others are distraught, frightened, and totally confused, because they realize that life is coming to an end.

A third group meets death with equanimity. The reasons are, however, very different: some are happy to be released soon from their physical suffering; others simply have deep trust that everything is also fine as it is. This latter attitude is the really meaningful one, because it makes it easier both for oneself and for relatives and friends to take leave.

If it is certain that no measures can be taken to prolong life, it is necessary to turn the tables and to consciously make use of the event. It is best not to connect impermanence with loss and suffering but with opportunities and freedom. Instead of giving in to the need for security and stability, one should understand death as a transition and to always be aware of how important the state of mind is. If one already accepts the fact of death during one's lifetime and does not suppress it, one lives more consciously in the here and now.

The easiest way to die is to dissolve the attachment to one's own body, to next of kin, and to possessions. Taking this into account also helps friends and family because, if a person close to the one who is dying clings too much, it is unpleasant for everybody. Things themselves do not experience happiness, and the joys brought forth by them are very inconsistent and useless in the grave. If one understands that, one will soon experience them as tools, but not cling to them.

A will that was written in a clear and beyond-personal moment for the lasting benefit of all, is already a relief during one's lifetime. In the end one does not know whether death comes unannounced or leaves sufficient time for preparations. If one dies suddenly, something written is available on which the offspring can rely. The more clearly everything is arranged and the better the assets distributed, the less the heirs quarrel. It is better, of course, if one can pass on one's property oneself with good wishes. To thank the friends and relatives in this way is meaningful for them and is a good basis for candid talks and a pleasant goodbye.

Generosity is liberating during the process of dying because one sheds mountains of luggage. If one has considered posterity and taken precautions for one's close ones or the continuation of one's work, it is much easier to part with this life. If one additionally wishes everybody as much good as possible, one experiences with relief that they won't need us any longer now and one can engage fully in the real thing, one's own death. Buddhists can also think that they will help the bereaved ones from the pure power-fields of the buddhas according to their ability or to get reborn in order to further enjoy the existing good bonds.

Bonds to family and friends, landscapes, world views, and experiences are often stronger than the attachment to possessions. But here one should know that they only reflect a few possibilities of the mind, which can experience even more without a body. The fact that something infinitely more beautiful will be experienced when one lets go and dies with a free mind should be internalized while still alive.

If one wants to find something against fear of loss, the pain of saying goodbye, and deadly seriousness, one does not have to look far. Everyone enjoys life's unexpected great moments full of courage, joy, love, surplus, foresight, etc. How would it be if they were our real state? Would it be imaginable that the sun always shines, only one doesn't notice it? That ordinary, mediocre or bad experiences are similar to impermanent clouds that pass by one's internal insight without real substance or lasting power? It would clearly be worthwhile to go on a journey of discovery through what is an unavoidable death with such an attitude to the timeless inherent richness of mind. Whoever, like Goethe, says in his final breath "More light!" knows what to look for.

It sets a good example to those around if the ones dying consciously use Buddha's advice and follow his meditations and thus can leave from here visibly relaxed and go with curiosity or excitement for the trip, rather than with fear. Their trust has been solidified over the years through their meditation and the wish to develop for the good of all beings, and attests to a life led meaningfully. That way one is also a good example for others, even in the final minutes of this life.

DEVELOPING FOR THE BENEFIT OF ALL

The human maturity that is often missing, despite the good education these days, comes from the culture of distraction. One is constantly caught by desires and sensations and does thousands of unimportant things. This leads to a distracted mind which rarely experiences "quality time." Everybody enjoys non-distracted, self-determined periods of time—that is why there is leisure time and vacation, but the goblin often comes along. In this way, the search for happiness in the outer world continues and the inner peace that actually brings happiness fails to appear. Even on their deathbed, most people do not manage to keep sight of what is essential. Skillful determination and strength are the key here, and these are acquired through meditation. Only the overcoming of one's own veils of stupidity, confusion, attachment, pride, or greed and the resulting patterns of lethargy and self-pity bring development.

There is a big, but familiar enemy here that has to be defeated totally: the notion that there might be a middle level of normality, between the rosy dreams above and the black-gray depressions below, on which one could rely. This error in reasoning was understandable in socialist countries, where much had been cut down to a meager standard for everybody and one wished for the masses little that was unmanageable and exuberant. For a true understanding of life and the nature of mind, this point of view is a self-built prison.

This "middle" level only exists in the conditioned world, and whoever is looking for something real and permanent should instead look first for the experiencer of things and be open to its fearlessness, joy, and love. Whoever works constantly for the benefit of all on this basis, and shares all the good that happens to him with others, will gradually realize that bad days seldom happen. Many valleys of the "unpleasant states of mind" have already been filled up through Buddha's practices and a joyful undisturbed state of mind will have constantly gained momentum and will thus directly appear for the dying person as timeless wisdom.

Whoever was honest, mature, and compassionate in his life, stylishly avoiding political correctness and constantly looking for the experiencer behind the experiences, has the possibility, when dying, to become one with the Clear Light that appears. This state of full realization is called enlightenment.

The bigger the confidence is in the teacher, in one's own abilities to work with mind, and in the nature of things, the easier it is to embark on the process of dying. The foundation here is the habit, built up through years of meditation practice, of consciously resting in indestructible space. It is actually wonderful when blessing, trust, and practice have become unshakable certainty and one is able to keep the teacher or a Buddha clearly in mind during the dissolution of the body. But other noble beyond-personal qualities pave the way to this experience for the dying one. Here courage should be mentioned first because one thus draws on good impressions that are firmly stored. In this way, one can freely admit oneself into death, rather than frantically lose against it in the end. If one realizes that everyone dies anyway and if one keeps the feeling of self-importance small, mind relaxes and there arises increasing joy and serenity.

The confidence that mind is ultimately indestructible space and that all perfection is simultaneously inherent in it, helps even to let pains run "alongside" and to perceive them as less real. Anyone who, in a state of absorption, experienced the joyful awareness that lies behind and between phenomena, dies fulfilled and, in the future and for the good of all beings, will choose realms of existence in which he can most effectively do useful things with friends from past lives and remove veils that still remain in mind.

Inner Preparation for Death

For everybody:	
●	**Recognizing impermanence in everyday situations**—during meals, every time when saying goodbye
●	**Accumulating good impressions in mind**—through meaningful actions
●	**Clarifying and dissolving difficulties**—forgiving and making good wishes
●	**Practicing letting go**—giving things away, writing a will, consciously saying goodbye to people, things and situations
●	**Concentrating on benefiting others**—taking oneself less and less seriously

For Buddhists:	
●	**Refuge**—the orientation toward the refuge gives safety and protection
●	**Listening to Buddha's teachings and understanding them**—recognizing the emptiness of all things and dealing with impermanence and death
●	**Bodhisattva promise**—securing the attitude to act for the benefit of all
●	**Developing devotion to the teacher**—recognizing one's own buddha nature through the teacher
●	**Meditation**—pacifying the mind and deepening the insight into how things are
●	**Practicing Phowa**—in order to be able to use death as a springboard to liberation

	The Outer Preparation for Death	
For everybody:	•	The actual art of dying means being calm and relaxed and staying undistracted and one-pointed at the same time.
	•	The dying person should imagine the most beautiful thing possible above his head and wish to go there.
	•	The friends should sit near the head of the bed.
	•	Everything that pulls the energy of the dying downward should be avoided (standing at the foot of the bed, foot-massages, pain in the lower body, etc.).
	•	focus on good things above the head
	•	as little distraction as possible
	•	instead of a constant coming and going of all kinds of people, restrict the visitors to important ones who are in a good mood, preferably at the beginning of the process of dying
For Buddhists:	•	Similar to when meditating, one should arrange the outer circumstances so that one is distracted by as few disturbances as possible.
	•	a bright, light room with a pleasant atmosphere and without TV, internet or other unnecessary influences
	•	pictures of the teacher, buddha forms or other sources of the refuge in the visual field, in order to remember what is essential
	•	pleasant surroundings with no agitation
	•	have a fixed time in the daily routine for meditations
	•	watch or listen to teachings in order to remember the teacher and the methods

OUTER PREPARATION FOR DEATH

The essential art of dying consists of being easy-going and relaxed while at the same time staying mentally undistracted and one-pointed. Therefore, the one who is dying should imagine the most beautiful thing above his head and wish to go there as often as possible (see "Terminal Care").

Family, friends and acquaintances should best sit near the head end. One should not stand at the foot end of the bed and give foot massages. If the terminally ill person has pain in the lower body that could pull his energy downward, he should get enough pain medication so that awareness is not stuck in this area but can focus on the top of the head. In other ways, as well, the body should experience as little distraction as possible.

Friends should not just come "whenever," but should be there at the beginning of the dying process, and only in a good mood. Instead of a constant coming and going of all imaginable beloved and less beloved ones, it makes sense to limit the visits to those who are essential. It is best if a close friend or relative takes care of this, according to an earlier agreement. It is easier for him to say no.

Just as when meditating, one should create the outer conditions in a way that one is distracted by as few disturbances as possible. During the last stage of dying, a clear, bright room without television, internet or other unnecessary influences, but with a pleasant mood, is the best. There should be enough space in the room in front of the dying person so that he readily breathes in deeply and has a light-hearted feeling.

For Buddhists, pictures of the teacher, the Red Buddha of Limitless Light, or other sources of refuge in his field of vision will constantly remind him of the essentials and help him.

A pleasant, not agitative, environment is always an advantage, and meditations should be integrated into the daily routine. One can also listen to recorded teachings. In this way, one is reminded of the teacher and the methods pointing to timeless mind. If Buddhist friends are around, they can call attention to the upcoming steps during the course of dying and, in doing so, accompany the process.

Of course, it is best if one's own teacher is present in the last moments or can shortly before prepare the one dying on his way. If this is not possible, the teacher is represented by his threefold power-field: by the blessing-field of his lineage, which condenses as soon as one thinks of him or just puts up a picture; by the connection he has with the one dying; and by the care-giving Buddhist friends and centers.

Posture During the Process of Dying

Consciousness usually leaves the body through one of the seven openings in the head or through the less favorable two—or three for women—in the lower body, but that is not demonstrated by the emptying of the bowel and bladder in dying. This happens because of muscle relaxation. Through these "karmic" body openings, the energy and the perception of the mind are guided again into a new birth within the conditioned world, while exit through the skull as with the Phowa and sometimes through the left nostril, may lead into a pure land. If one has not mastered liberating practices such as Conscious Dying, there are other methods that are beneficial for helping advance the mind through the body.

If one focuses on the left nostril, one should adopt the posture that Buddha used for this purpose at the time of his death near the "lucky city" Kushinagar in northeast India twenty-four hundred years ago. This body position is known as the *lion posture* and is the last of the twelve actions Buddha showed in his life for the good of all beings. It gives the one who is dying an increased clarity of mind, even without meditation and empowerment.

Here one turns to the right side. The legs are placed sideways on top of each other, the left hand lies on the thigh, and the fingers of the right hand press on the openings of the sensory organs in the head, if possible. Here the little finger presses on the mouth, the ring finger on the nostril, the middle finger on the eye, the index finger on the ear and the thumb on the right main artery. Thereby the energy of awareness will not escape through the right channel of activity, but can go into the left channel of wisdom. In this way, one experiences one's innate wisdom and leaves the body through the left nostril and, along with the appropriate attitude, can reach a higher state of consciousness.

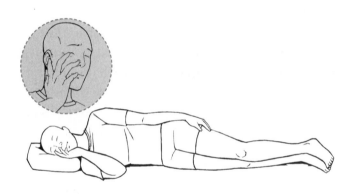

The lion posture [18]

It is easier and somewhat less inconvenient to sit as upright as possible when dying. Here one sits propped against pillows and imagines above one's head the most beautiful thing that can be experienced, with the wish to go there. If this is a state of bliss beyond all concept of ego, one goes the way to lasting happiness in this simple manner.

In 1986 in the Forbidden City of Beijing I saw, standing in a corner, a device that the Chinese were apparently not able to make use of. It looked like a wooden dental chair for very restless customers and made it technically possible to put pressure on all upper and lower body parts at the moment of death, leaving only the skullcap free—indicating a knowledge of Phowa.

In some Nepalese tribes it is the duty of the eldest son to smash the father's skullcap after his death. In Scandinavia, skulls can be found from the Stone and Bronze Ages whose holes, according to the researchers, are not explainable through the removal of tumors. No matter how good the technical skills of the people really were, they only had a supporting effect: if the emperor had done many bad things, mind would find its way only to the realm that corresponded to his actions, despite all the technology.

Again and again the question is asked whether one can meditate lying down. In general, one can also align the mind to a point in this position. However, without a doubt, it is much more effective when sitting because the inner magnetic field aligns with the Earth's axis and, among other things, one does not fall asleep so quickly. If one is not able to sit anymore because of lack of strength, it is best to imagine oneself sitting upright and to keep the familiar form of buddha or lama in the heart.

THE INNER EXPERIENCE OF
THE DYING PERSON

Everybody knows how bodies pass away. There is the sudden death, as in a heart attack or when, on two wheels with a lot of horsepower in the curve, one hits ice, loose gravel or bitumen. A medium-fast passing away is experienced when first one organ deteriorates and then another. Worldwide, often the quite prolonged and unpleasant processes of dying are caused mostly by hunger, old age, AIDS, and cancer.

However different these separations of body and mind look, in all cases exactly the same thing happens. The streams of awareness, which are running non-stop and are spread over energy wheels and channels in the living body, pull back into the central energy axis. During a medium-fast dying, in which one loses the connections to life within a reasonable period of time, the people in the surroundings recognize this process most clearly. But even in a complete destruction of a body, awareness hangs around for a while, experienced as "heart" or one's "own center." In what follows I will give the Tibetan explanation for the process of dying, referring to the many experiences of former meditation masters. One can track these processes well, and its rich experience becomes more and more precise through the growing knowledge of Western medicine.

EMERGING OF THE ELEMENTS

When our body came into existence, three conditions came together: the egg of our mother, experienced as red; the sperm from the father, appearing as white; and, our consciousness, which since beginningless time had built up the conditions for being born with a particular genotype, in a specific culture, and with certain parents. When these two cells became a body, the white light of the father moved from the heart center upward and since then is located on the cranial tip of the child. In the case of a daughter, the red light of the mother dwells at the "G-spot" a hand's width below the navel, whereas in the case of a son it rests at the prostate gland and when aroused, at the tip of his noble tool. The two lights form the endpoints of the central magnetic energy channel, which in turn develops energy wheels in five places, consisting of more channels and filling the body with enlightened energy. Those in the head control the body; those in the throat bless the speech. At heart level in the middle of the body they awaken the mind, in the navel the artistic qualities, and at the lowest point, they stimulate the activity.

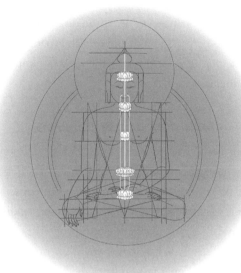

Body and energy system

The Human Body: Channels, Winds, and Elements

Although everything is ultimately mind, it is exciting how it expresses and also recognizes itself. Just as anatomy and physiology determine the Western understanding of the body, the imagination of numerous energy channels (72,000) and energy wheels (Tib. *tsa*), basic energies (Tib. *lung*) and essences (Tib. *thigle*) shape the Buddhist perspective on the body.

All worlds and all bodies of beings arise out of the five elements of earth, water, fire, wind and space. What is solid gives mass, what flows holds everything together, heat causes maturation, wind facilitates growth and mobility, and space forms the necessary field for development. According to the Buddhist teachings, a fetus emerges from the seed of the father, an egg cell of the mother, and a consciousness that is attracted by the karmic connection to parents and their environment. With conception the five elements give the human body its qualities and possibilities, and are directly related to its ability to perceive the inner world of experience and the outer surroundings.

The Buddhist who wants to experience his mind as joyful space and Clear Light can use the energy channels which condense into the five energy wheels. Here the three main channels play a pre-eminent role: the central channel (Tib. *uma*), the right side channel (Tib. *roma*), and the left side channel (Tib. *kyangma*).

The central channel runs from the top of the skull through the middle of the body to a place four fingers below the navel in the abdomen. It is connected to unseparated wisdom. It is "as thin as the shaft of an arrow," straight, hollow, lucid, and can have different colorations, according to the goal of the practice. The side channels are thinner than the central channel, end at the nostrils, and pull the energy of space from four hands' width in front of it, the energy of air from three hands' width, the energy of heat from two hands' width, and from a single hand's width that of liquid. At the nostrils themselves these four energies meet the solid state.

They run vertically downward, right and left next to the central channel, and enter back into the central channel four fingers below the navel. The right channel is red. It stands for methods or compassion and is male, while the white, wisdom-bearing left one expresses inspiration and wisdom.

The energies at the tip of the nose are used as raw material for realization. They contain the life energy and are closely related to the mind that "rides" on them, as the texts say. Therefore, calming the movement of energies leads to a stabilization of the mind, and one can influence the intensity of one's emotions by controlling the breath. An accomplisher masters the energies and winds, constantly transforms disturbances into wisdom, and keeps the energies into th central channel.

The essence spreads over the energy channels within the whole body and is the basis of life and awareness. It emerges at conception at heart level, out of the central channel, includes all five elements, and also contains the life energy. After fertilization it follows both the red mother-essence that moves downward and the white father-essence that rises upward.

Disturbing emotions condense in the channels as obstacles to the flow of energy and wind, and as a result the body or the outer world is experienced as unpleasant. But since all disturbances have their origin in ignorance of the nature of mind, here is also the starting point for liberation. The energies, winds and elements can be influenced through the numerous meditation practices (conscious breathing, focusing on beyond-personal light-energy forms, the reciting of mantras, and other practices, such as prostrations or *Phowa*), thus forming the basis for a direct path to enlightenment.

DISSOLVING OF THE ELEMENTS

During the course of dying, the process is reversed from what happened during the formation of the body and the expansion of its energy channels. Without the immense help of today's medicine, dying is usually accompanied by severe suffering, especially when the flow of vital energies calms down and the energy channels dissolve. Therefore, one can use painkillers in a conscious and appropriate way. On the one hand, one should have as little pain as possible; on the other hand, one should stay in the clearest consciousness possible.

In Buddhism, the body is understood as consisting of five elements. The gradual loss of control of them is described as their dissolution "into one another" or "into their essence." Here the dying person undergoes different experiences, which can be lived through either as very overwhelming or as liberating, depending on the content of mind.

During the entire course of dying, the experiences of the four elements of earth, water, fire and air fluently dissolve into one another again according their nature. Skin, bones, muscles, tendons, and everything solid form the earth; the various fluids such as blood, lymph, and semen belong to water; the body heat makes the fire; and the breathing corresponds to the element air. Consciousness, the fifth element, which breaks away from the body at death, belongs to space. The order and especially the duration of this dissolution can turn out very differently, depending on the karma. It can take days, weeks, or in rare cases even years. Because the senses lose their abilities during these processes, they are experienced more or less clearly.

Dissolving the Element Earth

When the consciousness of the dying person withdraws from solid to fluid, one loses control over the solid parts of the body. Muscle strength decreases considerably, the movements are erratic, and one feels heavy. One can no longer hold oneself upright, and the grip gets weak. One constantly has the feeling of falling; even though one is already lying down, one tries to cling to things and people. The abilities to move and to think clearly are lost. One can no longer keep the mind one-pointed, gets confused, and panics easily. Finally, one no longer knows whether the intellect is still reliable and starts to perceive delusions on the inner level. Depending on the nature of stored impressions, unbearably loud noises occur; some people have the feeling of being crushed by huge mountains. If one experiences a kind of flickering like hot air, that shows unmistakably that the dying has begun.

Dissolving the Element Water

Next, one loses the control of everything flowing in the body, which means that the water element changes into the fire element. Circulation gets increasingly weaker, and the involuntary muscle strength declines, so that one loses control of the tongue, and some also of the intestines and bladder. The nose runs; lips, mouth, and tongue are dry; and one has a strong sensation of thirst. Here, too, the quality of the experience depends on the stored impressions. Since now the mind is not working logically anymore, one tries to get along with the help of emotions. One focuses on something that one loves or which awakens deep feelings in oneself.

Some feel uncomfortable, becoming quickly irritated and easily angry. One has the impression of hearing the sound of thundering water, as if an ocean is approaching. At the same time one thinks that one is floating or being torn away by waves. An unambiguous sign of this phase is the experience of smoke-like phenomena that drift by and rise.

Dissolving the Element Fire

Thirdly, the body heat withdraws more and more from the outer parts of the body and into the center, which means that the fire element is dissolving into the wind element. One loses control of the heat balance and thus any feeling of warmth. The heart is no longer able to pump the available blood to the remote areas. Medically speaking, this is the so-called centralization of the circulation. The extremities (toes, fingers, legs and arms) become anemic, pale, and cold. The body cools down more and more from the bottom up, and the breath gets shorter. One has a vague feeling of openness. Although one tries to focus on the feeling of love or a beautiful memory, it all slips away again and again. Everything appears strangely hollow and meaningless, and confusion increases significantly. The surrounding world becomes blurred and the consciousness fluctuates heavily. At times, one is clear and present; at other times, confused or unconscious. Flickering red lights—similar to sparks or fireflies—may appear.

Dissolving the Element Wind

Finally, the wind element dissolves into consciousness, and one loses the last sensation of the surrounding world. One has more and more difficulties with breathing, and the feeling of shortness of breath can be relieved neither through quick breathing nor through intense assistance of the accessory respiratory muscles. With increasing exhaustion, the ability to willfully assist in breathing declines, and one has the feeling of being crushed by a huge load.

Deeply uprooted and no longer able to fight, one is ready to give up all ideas about oneself and the world. Since the composure of consciousness decreases, the control of bodily functions now also dissolves completely. This leads to cramps, often followed by leakage of urine and a bowel movement. But this does not mean that the awareness is leaving the body here. The respiratory and circulatory centers in the brain stem are completely damaged by the oxygen deficiency. In the end one breathes in deeply two more times and breathes out one very long last time. Then respiratory and cardiac arrest also occurs.

On the inner level one sees flickering lights, like candles in the wind. The wind element dissolves into space with the last breath. With it, all the sensory impressions end. That means that one does not see, hear, taste, smell, or feel anything anymore. At this time death is medically confirmed.

Energies in Death

The above-mentioned experiences emerge mainly because of the energies that were spread throughout the seventy-two thousand channels in the body. But to put the reader's mind at ease, for people with good stored impressions—especially with a sudden death, during sleep, or with pain medication—these experiences are rarely undergone as completely or as strongly as described here.

In dying, the energies withdraw more and more into the central magnetic axis of the body. First, they stream into the five power wheels of head, neck, body center at heart level, navel center, and the lower place of power in the body. Subsequently, when the power wheels dissolve, their energy fields melt into the central channel itself. Here the non-meditator experiences a weakening of the sensory impressions. A feeling grows that something is there, but one does not know exactly what. One sees something, but cannot recognize what it is. It all sounds like a mumbling, and one does not understand the words any more. The lack of clarity of these perceptions shows that the consciousness, which in an awake state works through all the senses, is withdrawing more and more into the central channel. When this happens, many are deeply frightened, as though one is hearing thousands of thunderclaps at the same time. The Tibetans say that at this moment in the heart of the dying something breaks and three small drops of liquid jump out. The separation of consciousness from the body is frightening only for those who are untrained because it is unknown. If one is not prepared for what is happening, intense fear can occur. The person who thought of others during life and therefore basically expects something good, or has heard these teachings and has meditated a lot, can recognize everything and keep the mind calm or even meet his teacher or a familiar buddha.

The point of time when respiratory and cardiac arrest occurs is seen as the moment of death from a medical perspective. This, however, is accurate only from a superficial perspective. It is true that the exchange with the outside world is over, the heart doesn't beat any longer, and the active metabolism—the emitting of carbon and the absorbing of oxygen—dries up. Also, in the brain stem no further activity can be detected. But the consciousness of the dying person is still active, and the connection to the body is not yet completely separated.

DYING CONTINUES

Even when the process of dying seems to be completed as seen from the outside, inside the body metabolic processes and brain waves still take place for twenty to thirty minutes.[19] That is why only after this time do the outer signs of death manifest, such as rigor mortis and livor mortis. From a Buddhist point of view, death has occurred for everyone only when the heart center gets cold.

This subtle dissolution of the energies after the onset of death is called internal respiration. It takes place in three phases: appearance, increase, and attainment.

For people without meditation experience, but with little attachment, a little more than a half-hour after death some blood or mucus appears at one of the nine existing orifices, or the mouth opens. If the bowel and bladder empty during the dying process, this does not necessarily indicate that mind leaves the body here. In this case, the cause is the loss of body control. Similar signs may appear up to four days later, this time as a result of a strong attachment to life, which holds mind in the body for so long. At this point, however, every consciousness finally leaves the body. Exceptions to this are the deeply impressive abilities of meditation masters who can consciously keep and direct their energies beyond death (see "The Art of Dying").

Appearance: Liberation from Anger

As soon as the energies have withdrawn into the central channel of the body and circulation and breathing have stopped with clinical death, the movements of consciousness in the central channel begin. The white male energy from the sperm of the father, which during life rested at the crown of the head, now descends from the place approximately the width of eight fingers behind the original hairline to the heart level in the center of the body. This takes between ten and fifteen minutes. The metabolic processes of the brain come to a standstill and lead, except in extreme cold, to its dying-off.

Here, thirty-three feelings, memories, and ideas that are caused by hatred and anger gradually dissolve into awareness because disturbing emotions are ultimately nothing but energy-charged thoughts. For some people the experiencer, surrounded by a mild and moonlike light, moves through a tunnel toward something infinitely beautiful and meaningful, while others perceive a white glow. In the process many hear a long drawn-out sound like "haaaang." The consciousness of the one who is dying is now fully awake and on the way to the heart and will relive important experiences and digest impressions of people who were close to him. The fact that one experiences them again, as one had known them, shows the power of our memory. It does not at all mean that they have stayed in a timeless space and did not develop any further like everyone else. Because of strongly shared experiences, one will sooner or later meet again and in the usual range of emotions, but in new bodies and under new circumstances. Since in this process the notion of time also dissolves, the entire past life can pass by in fast motion during the five minutes in which the brain still remains intact at normal temperature.

The previous impressions are often described in near-death experiences, and there are a number of books on the subject, which are mentioned in the appendix. The impressions about to be described here are no longer experienced by the already-destroyed brain of the deceased, but are experienced by mind, directly and without concepts. Therefore, these experiences do not appear in the descriptions of near-death experiences, but rather are remembered, understood, and explained only by high lamas. Some meditators recall their boundless joy in the next life, and highly realized yogis know the condition from the state of absorption or from the experiences that they have had accompanying the deceased through these processes.

My wife Hannah and I received these teachings from our teachers: towering above everyone else, the 16th Gyalwa Karmapa, as well as Shamar Rinpoche, Situ Rinpoche, Jamgön Kongtrul Rinpoche, Gyaltsab Rinpoche, Ayang Tulku, Lopön Tsechu Rinpoche, Urgyen Tulku, Kalu Rinpoche, Tenga Rinpoche, Khyentse Rinpoche, Kanjur Rinpoche, Dudjon Rinpoche, Drigung Khandro, Dalai Lama, and other senior lamas and meditation masters.

Increase: Liberation from Attachment

After the white light has reached the heart level in the center of the body, the red light of the mother, which comes from the egg during fertilization, moves upward. It breaks away from the center of the body a handbreadth below the navel, and it, too, reaches the heart center within a period of ten to fifteen minutes.

During this increase, the center of consciousness in the stomach stops functioning. The importance of this nerve center in the abdomen, also called the solar plexus, should not be underestimated: ten times more commands and messages go from the belly to the head than vice versa, and its state largely determines the moods of its owner. Meanwhile tremendous bliss is experienced, beyond anything that was possible during life. An overwhelmingly beautiful warm red light, similar to a dreamlike sunset, appears and ascends, and many hear a sound like a deep syllable "aaaah."

Mind releases itself here from its strongest attachment: that of one's own body. Thus forty kinds of clinging and desire automatically disappear. All attachment to one's former life vanishes, wishes for worldly happiness have no object, and relationships that were established with people, places and experiences disappear. It is the end of expectations and constraints.

Attainment: Liberation from Dullness

Twenty to thirty minutes after cardiac arrest, when the energies of father and mother merge at heart level, every experience stops; there is only awareness. Seven veils resulting from ignorance disappear, and everything goes black and silent.

This darkness is the actual separation of consciousness from this life. Meeting this energy brings all concepts and disturbing emotions to an end. This zero-state is much shorter than the preceding movements, and ends at the moment in which mind shows itself in all its power of radiance.

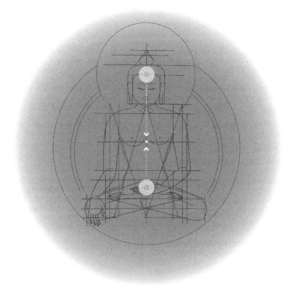

Appearance, increase, attainment

How can we use this knowledge about the inner processes of dying?

In the best scenario, one first learns about death by assisting a loved one, before one has to meet this challenge oneself. The clear idea of the processes brings security and confidence during the caring for another—and then later in one's own death. Therefore, in the next chapter the dying process will be described from the perspective of the family and nurses. The Buddhist views and methods enable all participants to bring out the best from this situation.

How the intermediate state looks as soon as the mind leaves the body and how one can also use this time consciously is described further in the following chapter.

Dissolution of the Elements: Body

element	solidity ▮▮▮▯▯	liquid ▮
dissolution	• dissolving of the earth element into the water element • navel center dissolves • visual consciousness decreases	• dissolving of the water element into the fire element • heart center dissolves • aural consciousness decreases
experience	• growing sensation of heaviness • unclear perception • one has the feeling of falling • unclear, confused, dull • one easily gets into a panic • sometimes one hears unbearably loud sounds and feels crushed *fire-accompanying wind*	• dryness • insatiable thirst • one only hears faintly and unclearly • one only sees things as from a distance • one hears the sound of roaring water and feels like floating • discomfort, restlessness, tempestuousness • tendency to get angry *life-carrying wind*
inner experience	• the feeling of being vanishes • logical thinking fades • apathy • short dream-like perceptions • light flickering *(like a mirage)* *equalizing wisdom*	• cognitive ability gets weaker and weaker • loss of mental clarity • memories fade • mind can get excited and confused • strong habits and impressions gain influence • one tries to be oriented by using emotions • things appear to be unreal • smoke-like appearances *mirror-like wisdom*
outer signs	*Control of solidity wanes:* • often obvious turmoil • facial color pales • eyes sink considerably deeper • loss of physical strength • movements become unclear • digestion stops • extremities become cooler and less sensitive	*Control of liquid wanes:* • no more voluntary movements • blood pressure gets weaker • body loses liquids, dries out • eyes, lips, mouth and tongue are dry • language weakens and finally stops • reduced eye-movements or eyes become mostly closed • increasing sleepiness • leakage of liquids
support for self	• sit upright or lie in lion's posture • let go of the past • meet death fearlessly • have intention of meeting Buddhism anew, to realize enlightenment • hold and calm mind • carry positive thoughts • commence preparation for *Phowa*	• think clearly and beneficially • think of love or loved ones • remember good relationships • imagine everything beautiful above oneself and develop the deep wish to go there • concentrate on the lama above oneself • start *Phowa* for oneself
support for others	• provide peace and direction	• give liquids

heat	air/wind
• dissolving of the fire element into the wind element • speech center dissolves • olfactory consciousness decreases	• dissolving of the wind element into space • activity center dissolves • gustatory and tactile consciousnesses decrease
• feeling of shortness of breath • increasing sensation of cold • surroundings fade • consciousness fluctuates a lot • body-sensations dissolve: pain, and well-being, heat and cold appear simultanuously • vague feeling of openness and dissolution • lightness * *downward-moving wind*	• end of all sense perceptions and connection to surroundings • one loses the last contact to the physical world • sometimes one is deeply frightened • one doesn't fight anymore and surrenders being somebody • relaxation * *pervasive wind*
• termination of the memory function *(i.e. although one tries to direct oneself to the feeling of love or a memory, everything slips away again)* • intense confusion • everything appears as being hollow and meaningless • flickering red lights, similar to fire embers in the wind or fireflies * *discriminating wisdom*	• mind can get into deep confusion, including hallucinations, depending on the previous experiences as being peaceful or threatening • all energy withdraws from the 72,000 channels into the central channel • energy essence breaks away from the heart • consciousness breaks away from the body • flickering lights, similar to a torch or flickering glow * *all-pervading wisdom*
Control of heat wanes: • further centralization of the bloodstream, beginning collapse of cardiac cycle • body heat recedes from the outer parts of the body toward the center, i.e., the extremities get pale and cold • breathing gets shallow, irregular • unclear, fragmentary consciousness *(i.e. first, clear and present; then, confused and unconscious)* • reactions are reduced or hardly visible	*Control of wind wanes:* • rattling breath • exhaling becomes longer than inhaling • respiratory failure *(i.e. last breathing-out, without breathing in again)* • cardiac arrest • finally clinical death occurs
• pacify one's mind • focus on the lama above oneself • start *Phowa*	• whoever has meditated a lot can keep his mind calm and has huge possibilities of development • all three possibilities of *Phowa* are possible now See "The Crucial Moment"
• cover lightly • always remind the dying person of everything beautiful above his head and to strengthen the wish to go there	• create good last impressions • when clinical death has occurred, start with *Phowa* for others • ensure that the dead person remains undisturbed for 30 to 40 minutes

Dissolution of the Energies: Consciousness

energy	male energy	female energy
dissolution	• essence of father dissolves in the cranium at the top of the central channel and streams towards the heart center • appearance dissolves into increase	• essence of mother dissolves at a point four fingers' width below the navel at the lower end of the central channel and rises up toward the heart center • increase dissolves into attainment
experience	• mind gets more subtle and refined • one has the impression of moving through a tunnel & experiences a very clear white light • one hears the sound *"HANG"* • 33 mental states *(e.g. hatred, anger, rage, aversion, fear, etc.)* dissolve and one experiences profound clarity • strong correspondence with near-death experiences	• ascending of the female energy causes heat and experiences of warm, reddish light • one hears the sound *"AH"* • 40 mental states *(e.g. attachment, desire, expectation, etc.)* dissolve and one experiences great bliss
inner experience	**appearance** (Tib. *nang*): • appearance of a white light *(beautiful, clear, mild moonlight)* • the ability inherent in mind shows itself in ways including the extensive memory of previous lives	**increase** (Tib. *ched*) • glow of a slight reddish light *(sunlight on a cloudless morning sky)* • experience of unconditioned joy
outer signs' medical explanations	*about 5 to 10 minutes after the clinical death* • irreversible functional loss of the cranial brain centers *(cell junctions of the central nervous system and the nerve cells themselves)*	*about 10 to 15 minutes after the clinical death* • irreversible functional loss of the "belly-brain" *(i.e. the peripheral nerve network—ganglia—in the abdomen)*
preparation and recommendations for behavior	• clear intention and the wish to use the dying process for the benefit of all beings and to reach liberation or enlightenment: things exercised in refuge meditation and giving and taking meditation • liberation from all aversion: one of the things exercised in Loving Eyes meditation • letting go of the past and opening up to space: things exercised in Diamond Mind meditation	• dissolution of all attachment, insight into the complexity of all phenomena, and relaxation: things exercised in the Foundational Practices of the mandala offerings
	Emanation State of the Buddha (Skt. *Nirmanakaya*) can be experienced	Joy State of the Buddha (Skt. *Sambhogakaya*) can be experienced

male and female energies	Clear Light
• male and female energies melt in the heart • actual death • attainment dissolves into space	• dissolving of all energies • space dissolves into Clear Light
• melting of both energies with the inner awareness causes the experience of total darkness and "tranquility" with absolutely no sense perceptions • 7 mental states *(e.g. ignorance, dullness, etc.)* dissolve	• extremely clear, radiant light
attainment (Tib. *thob*) • vivid dark appearance *(cloudless sky without sun, moon and stars)* • stiff ideas and mental limitations dissolve • separation between subject and object dissolve	• the true nature of mind is experienced or one faints, followed by the bardo of suchness
about 20 to 30 minutes after the clinical death • irreversible functional loss of the cardio-muscular cells in union • appearance of the outer signs of death: rigor mortis, livor mortis, white and red liquids excrete from orifices *(mouth, nose, ears)*; this can fail to appear, however, if the body is too strongly destroyed	• facial features relax
• melting phase in meditations • mahamudra absorption	• letting go of all previous experiences • recognizing the clear light as an expression of mind • easing off of the tendency to grasp • resting relaxed in what is • Phowa into the truth state
Truth State of the Buddha (Skt. *Dharmakaya*) can be experienced	Consciously experiencing and resting in the Clear Light (Tib. *Tudam* meditation)

TERMINAL CARE

While the moment of death is nowadays clearly defined from a medical perspective (i.e. as brain death and irreversible termination of life in a biological sense as the brain stem ceases its function), different time frames and states in the process of dying are understood, depending on culture and world view. The way of viewing life, health and the approach to death have been in constant change over the centuries. Because of child mortality, crop failures, wars and epidemics in the late Middle Ages and early modern times, death was a familiar part of everyday life. Death and life were ever-present and intertwined not only because more often than today one could dwell among the dead by an accident or misfortune, but also because the dying ones were cared for and nursed at home until they died. In almost all societies, death was considered to be a journey into another world, for which one was to prepare already during life. Dying was a conscious preparation for the approaching death, both for the person who was dying and for the community, and began with the first signs of decline. Except in the case of war or epidemic, one rarely died alone; friends, neighbors, and relatives gathered around the bed to support the dying person. Death was not only the end but always also a new beginning, for which one wanted to prepare. In many cultures, the condition of a person in his hour of death was seen as crucial for his future destiny. It was therefore important to be ready in time and to reflect on future events so that one could prepare oneself.

With industrialization and the progress of medicine in the nineteenth century, the attention in the West shifted subtly from a dying person to a dying body. Little by little, one discovered life-prolonging methods that were associated with stays in hospitals and unfamiliar nurses. The surroundings became colder, often impersonal, and goal-related. The division of the tasks into various professional branches also changed the relationship with the one who was dying or dead. One example of this is the introduction of the impersonal administrative act of the death certificate, in which the exact time and cause of death are registered by a doctor who is usually unknown, while relatives are hardly involved. Another example is the professional funeral industry, which takes over all tasks for the family after death, such as washing and dressing the body and taking charge of the obituary, the funeral ceremony, etc.

GRACEFULLY TAKING LEAVE

If at the deathbed one experiences the remnant of a formerly flourishing person, heavily changed through medication or decay, one definitely dislikes seeing that. One wants to be constructive and affirming, but does not really know how. The way to manage this is to understand the indestructibility of the buddha nature in everyone and to recognize that all the meaningful things that the dying person previously accomplished in his life are still with him and constitute his essential nature. This view produces a graceful attitude toward the dying person as well as for the dying process itself. The various radio programs are still running, but the receiver (the body) only manages to pass on some scratchy sounds to the world. But, at the same time, mind itself is like timeless space which, all-encompassing and unchanging, generates everything. It cannot die or disappear because it had neither come to be nor was composed of anything. What one sees as decaying and dying is only the body, and one clings to it strongly until death. If, as a companion of a beloved wonderful person, one knows that nothing can be lost and that, after maturation in the intermediate state, the tendencies accumulated in the store-consciousness of mind will appear again in the next life, one can relax. As a Buddhist, one adapts to the fact that the dying process leads to a new rebirth—in a way one is witnessing the beginnings of a new packaging of mind in a container that will hopefully bring happiness.

So that the farewell of the relatives from the dying person does not get too painful, it helps both sides to prepare for it. It is wise for the dying person to wish everyone everything good and to slowly but surely say goodbye to his family, friends and possessions. It is encouraging and often helps to round off the relationship by joyfully remembering all the good and meaningful things that one has learned and shared. Then all can move on freely.

The dying person should forgive the difficult people and, in that way, dissolve the bond to them in order not to meet them again in the next life. The best self-protection in this situation is to consciously let go of all feelings of revenge and guilt and to also forgive oneself. The insight that everything bad ultimately happens out of ignorance and not out of ill will—and will bring corresponding results for the causer—should make this crucial step easier. Dissolving negative feelings and making good wishes is equally important for the dying person and the loved ones.

If one is able, at least conceptually, to see the process of dying like changing one's clothes, it becomes easier for everybody. After a life lived together, one surely shares lasting insights and experiences and this creates the opportunities to meet again in future lives. What one now thinks of one another, how one meets, and what one wishes for others—all of this essentially shapes the common future. To consciously orient oneself to happiness and to what is important creates surplus and really makes sense in the long term.

One should absolutely support that the dying person is not being kept away from what is essential by unnecessary and superficial issues. Instead of getting lost in petty memories, it is necessary to kindly and generously clarify everything, to let go of all that is disturbing, as well as is possible, and then to focus on the liberation of the now constricting and aching body. It is more important to deal with the nature of mind and to understand that it is beyond death and birth. One prepares the dying for going in the best way possible by reminding him again and again that the most beautiful thing ever imaginable is above the top of his head and that he wants to go there. The trick is not to take the whole affair personally, since every being will die sooner or later.

THE SIX LIBERATING ACTIONS

Many people hope that death may occur as late as possible, and then painlessly and without disease: watching TV, falling asleep, breathing out, over. But if one reads the obituaries or looks into the hospitals, one quickly realizes that only a few have that experience. According to statistics, only a low percentage of the population has such conditions.[20] Most people die slowly, and often much more consciously than they wished. According to surveys, nine out of ten people in the West want to die at home surrounded by their family. However, reality looks different; only very few actually succeed in this. Some people manage to spend the end of their life in a humane hospice. Today most people die in the hospital or nursing home.

If one wants to care for people in their last days, weeks, months, or even years, new challenges always arise. Under such circumstances, it is helpful to have an orientation, a fixed guideline which gives a liberating direction to everything that happens. A meaningful attitude helps and enriches others as well as oneself, but one also needs the corresponding methods in order to hold the view. Buddha summarized them in six activity fields: generosity, vast and meaningful action, patience, enthusiastic action, meditation, and wisdom. He called them the *six paramitas* or liberating actions. Whoever embeds them into his everyday life will appear neither strange nor sentimental, but rather will become an unshakable pillar for everybody. Connected with the ultimate view that everything affects everything else and is part of the same totality, these actions work naturally and are highly liberating. With regular application they dissolve the separation between actor, receiver, and the surrounding world, until it is simply natural to be useful and to do good things.

An action can be liberating and enlightening only in connection with the insight, or instantaneous experience, that the experiencer, that which is experienced, and the experience itself are without any lasting nature of their own and are part of the same totality.

Buddha taught that every moment of life—be it in the most beautiful experiences of courage and love, in daily life, and even while dying—can lead to realization through the liberating or "going-beyond" actions. While meaningful actions themselves help others as well as oneself, they are only liberating when the experienced separation between the actor, object, and receiver falls away. Only the dissolution of this habit by the insight into the emptiness of an existing nature of its own and the recognition of the mutual dependency of everything that happens unfolds all the richnesses of mind. This happens through the sixth and ultimate stage of the liberating actions—wisdom.

With this view of wisdom, the five basic meaningful

actions have the effect of being liberating or even enlightening, and every encounter with beings and the world is a welcome field of application on the way. Then everything pleasant is a blessing—something good that one can share with others—and one experiences all difficulties as a teaching and the dissolution of bad karma.

Only by storing meaningful and useful actions along with words, and by realizing wisdom, is enlightenment attained. Therefore, it is consequential that both the dying person and the caregivers actually use the time of goodbye for the accumulation of good impressions.

In what follows, the essential points that Buddha has advised for all areas of life, without wagging his finger, in order to be generally beneficial in dealing with others will be described—assistance that can well be applied during terminal care.

Six Liberating Actions		
❶	Generosity	generosity short-term, long-term and ultimate —with body, speech and mind
❷	Vast and Conscious Action	acting, speaking and thinking in a way that brings happiness
❸	Patience	endurance, perseverance, tenacity
❹	Enthusiastic action or diligence	doing something meaningful for others without expectation
❺	Meditation	creating a distance from what appears in mind
❻	Wisdom	experience of the timeless indestructible experiencer

Generosity

Nothing brings beings closer to one another than simple signs which express sympathy and the wish to do good for others: just generosity. Thus one affirms the richness that is inherent in space and the useful qualities that beings possess. From within this situation, giving is easy because it is fulfilling and part of a totality. In the traditional texts one distinguishes between three kinds of giving:

To be generous with food, money, or time, especially when one can directly ensure the survival of others.

Generous behavior also refers to everyday life. One gives time, love, and trust and enjoys the hours that are shared.

In terms of terminal care, generosity means to enrich the last period of life for a seriously ill or dying person. Here it is important to pay attention to his needs rather than to suffocate him with an over-caring siege. Moments of immediate openness are particularly valuable. They give strength, honor the relationship, and enrich all involved. Tears and grief, on the other hand, are no help for the dying person; they will rather distract and burden him. It is better to use the emerging feelings for care and clear exchange, thus providing security for the dying person. This facilitates the transition from life to death and makes sense.

To provide protection to others, but above all, a meaningful education and training.

This helps them for a lifetime. Long-term assistance also belongs here as well, such as supporting strict limits on the birth rate in poor countries of the world, in order to enable both children and parents to lead a life of dignity.

Protection in the case of terminal care might mean arranging all practical matters for the dying person, so that he gets the calming feeling that everything is really all right. One also helps him to write his will, arrange his papers, and keep difficult relatives or business partners from making annoying visits, so that he is not kept from essential matters by unnecessary and unpleasant issues. Instead of talking about trivial things, it is much more important to give the dying person time to consciously bid farewell to everything material and to all his friends. He can break away from this life a lot more easily when he has consciously distributed his belongings to friends while still alive.

The gift of the liberating teachings of Buddha.
Pointing to beginningless mind, the teachings encompass this life, dying, the death that follows, and all rebirths until enlightenment. The spots in the mirror of mind that became clear through this knowledge can also be easily linked to this level in future lives, until the goal—the fully realized human being—is achieved. That is why sharing the teachings counts as the highest form of generosity. If one is able to convey to the dying person that his mind is bound to this decaying body only for the present life span, it is calming. If one adds that mind is beyond death and birth, like space, emerging appearances of confusion and aging become more acceptable. This view confers the often missing dignity on the last part of life. It helps the dying to increasingly relax, and oneself to face one's own death more fearlessly.

Vast and Meaningful Action

Through generosity there emerges openness and trust, which one best ensures with meaningful behavior. The impressions that one plants in the store-consciousness during life are the only thing that follows one after death and shape further experiences and rebirths. To do, speak and think that which brings happiness, therefore, has the highest meaning and quickly produces an unshakeable mind. Through further practice, one can even liberate oneself completely from superficial disturbing emotions.

How could this look at the sickbed?

It is most important to eliminate the causes of disturbances. Not only by observing one's own behavior as caregiver and using the ten meaningful actions, but, above all, by providing a good, calm environment.[21] Discussions with doctors or nurses do not belong here, just like derogatory comments or the latest family gossip. Instead of judging the behavior of others or constantly questioning the doctor and nurse, one should be in friendly cooperation and always emphasize the good qualities of others, while one happily lets the whiners and squabblers come to nothing. Nursing the dying person should take place in the background and not be in the foreground. It is more important to constantly emphasize all the good from his life and to make him an example for all. This gives meaning and strength to his situation.

If one keeps the overview and, at the same time, does something meaningful that rounds off his life, this is a great gift. One has to have maturity in order to really put into practice these recommendations of supporting a beloved person. At the beginning, one often clumsily stands around for a long time—wants to help but is not allowed or is unable to. But the benefit here is great. Through that, one develops a thick skin, which also allows one to fearlessly stay in one's own center in future difficulties.

Practical Recommendations for Caregivers, Families and Relatives

- Creating a pleasant, clean, quiet environment without much distraction works out best with a joyful, conscious attitude. One should also enjoy the surroundings oneself because the dying person will feel that. Before shifting the furniture one should sit down briefly and experience the room as a totality.

- The people sitting closest to the dying person should be real friends and have already resolved old bad feelings.

- If possible, one always sits at the head of the bed of the dying, not at his feet, and touches, if anything at all, only his upper body, his hand and the top of his skull.

- One cares for the dying person as calmly as possible, is aware of the meaning of what is happening, makes no unnecessary sounds, movements or physical contact, and makes no conversation.

- At this time any uncertainty and any artificial expression of emotion from the ones present are experienced as very disturbing. If at the deathbed one thinks more about the inheritance than about the situation of the dying, one should not be present. On the other hand, through compassion & conscious presence one can be of great benefit for the dying.

- Because the auditory sense is the last connection to the world of senses, mantras are very useful. Everybody with trust can whisper "OM AMI DEWA HRIH" into the ear of the dying or blow this mantra on one's own fingertips and then slightly touch the top of the skull of the dying. In this way one puts the power field of the Buddha of Limitless Light there.

- The dead body should not be touched during the first 30–60 minutes after the last breathing-out; one should not make any unnecessary sounds, so that the inner process of dying can proceed undisturbed.

- The dead should be left in the room and touched as little as possible—or even better not at all—for three days, if possible, but at least one hour after the examination of the corpse. Only then should one start with washing and dressing. If necessary one can arrange a final meeting with the family members, before the corpse is taken away. The climatic conditions and local laws do not always permit this liberty, and one should follow them. The first thirty to sixty minutes are the most important.

- Private and particularly cherished things should not be used, cleared away or given away for forty-nine days, if possible. If after the passing away everything is divided, thrown away or even argued about, this can lead to confusion and strong aversion for the deceased, which is harmful for the rebirth.

- One should only talk nicely about the dead and be generous in his name. Among other things, this can be gifts of money to several friends, people in need of help or non-profit organizations that were important to the dead.

Buddhist Methods for Caregivers, Families and Relatives

- At an early stage one should give blessing pills, nectar from empowerments, and the like to dying ones who are Buddhists or open to the teachings. Taken with trust, they bring—as a method of "liberation through taste"—a short-term mental improvement, a good rebirth or even liberation.

- Pictures of buddhas or altars should be at the head of the bed, because they pull the inner energies upwards and so help the dying to be reborn in a liberated or at least meaningful realm.

- One may, as often as the dying one wishes, recite the accompanying meditations and wishes, or play them on an audio-device next to the ear of the dying.

- After the last breathing-out one then can even sing or speak loudly all wishes and corresponding meditations. If the caregiver is able to do the meditation of Conscious Dying, the Hook of Compassion (*Phowa*; see "Conscious Dying"), which takes the mind of others into the Pure Land of Highest Bliss, the best time to do this meditation is 20–30 minutes after the last breathing-out. Blessed items can be put between the pillow and the top of the head of the dying/deceased; blessing strings, protector knots, etc. can be burnt with him or buried lying on his chest.

- The bereaved can put up pictures of the Buddha of Limitless Light in places where the deceased liked to be, because he will return to his favorite places again.

- One makes wishes and meditations in his name, donates to Buddhist centers or installs Buddhist libraries, puts up Buddha statues in the name of the dead or erects a stupa.

Patience

Good impressions that have been built up by previous meaningful actions can be instantly dissolved by anger and rage, and one gets lonely. When applied skillfully, patience and understanding are very effective antidotes to anger.

In the course of dying, the foundation for a good rebirth can be disturbed by anger and, in the case of very angry people, even destroyed. It is better to avoid this feeling at all costs. Both for dying ones as well as for the caregivers, it is of great advantage in this period of life to have practiced the antidotes for it. The earlier one discovers the feeling that flares up, the better one can narrow it down. Once recognized, one should create a distance on both sides, without dwelling on the anger in detail or acting rashly. Best is to simply "freeze" it, either saying nothing else or saying something completely different.

If, however, the caregiver loses his patience or gets angry because a difficult behavior is continuously repeated—or if, over a very protracted illness, one gets the impression of being used— it is best to remember the previous days spent together. Then one brings to mind the frustration and the vulnerable state of the sick person and his pains, which keep him from controlling himself. In this way, one again develops more patience and compassion. Since these qualities are at the same time important raw material for one's own realization, one can actually be grateful to the nagging patient for the task. All difficult feelings and ideas that may arise at the deathbed—such as impatience, time pressure, incomprehension, boredom, uncertainty, and a lot more—lose their grip if one keeps track of the situation and stays aware: a human being is dying here! All things considered, a short break might easily help. Before one no longer recognizes anymore what a great gift one is just giving, and at the same time receiving, as development and good karma, one should call others in to take over—and then take care of the terminally ill person again, with freshness and surplus. Whoever, as caregiver, is able to avoid feeling exploited or attacked, makes it possible for the dying person to more easily access his own strength and maturity. With a clear head, one blocks any space for disturbing feelings.

As described, during a certain period in the course of dying anger may come up for the dying one for a while. If one has practiced for a long time through meditation and, above all, through mantras such as **OM MANI PEME HUNG** to simply not take one's own trips and those of the others seriously, then one will also find sufficient distance in this situation. One best lets the anger that emerges in the terminally ill about "unfair suffering" as understandable come to nothing. If necessary, with kindness and humor, one should make it clear to the sick person that sickness, old age, and death are nothing personal, but hit everybody and many are a lot worse off. One can also advise the dying one to concentrate on his breath, on a picture that inspires confidence, or on a buddha. If he is familiar with taking refuge, disturbing emotions will quickly dissolve again, because the buddha forms transmit favorable feedback experiences and he will end up melting with their light bodies. One can distract non-Buddhists from anger with beautiful notions or memories.

The point is to bring forth good impressions and to let the difficult feelings pass through unnoticed. The long periods of resting and waiting can also be used simply for further education, so one never runs out of topics for conversation, and as caregiver, one has advantages when one can turn toward the world again.

Enthusiastic Action

To do meaningful things for others without expecting anything for it, but simply because it is helpful and right, gives a protective power-field and makes body and speech into diligent helpers for the good that one wants to put into the world. With an attitude that takes real joy in meaningful actions and tirelessly protects and enriches, disturbing emotions and even pain mostly bounce off. One has more important things in mind!

If one stays sitting at the bedside and takes care of the dying friend or relative, even if one is dead tired oneself, a very fulfilling bond emerges beyond the pain barrier: To be actively engaged for the benefit of others creates a strength that can be used in other meaningful circumstances. It is "deeply" right and feels so good that it almost makes one addicted. From experience, it takes frequent meditations or a cool head to steer this strength meaningfully. If the dying one feels that somebody is doing something for him that is beyond measure, great thankfulness arises on his part and one strengthens the connections for future lives.

Also, even if he is physically at the end, the dying person still has speech and mind enough to be able, perhaps, to transmit valuable worldly wisdom. If others find the breadth of mind and the surplus to listen to him, it becomes a matter of accepting this gift with gratitude.

Meditation

At the end of life one realizes above all how useful it is to have meditated and built up deep convictions during life. At this time, one cannot train the mind anymore, but will certainly harvest the fruits. When meditating, it is all about creating a distance to what appears in mind, plays around in it, is perceived by it, and then dissolves there again. If one has observed this process often enough during the state of absorption, one will gradually be able to apply to everyday life the freedom gained in this way.

When the energies increasingly withdraw during dying, the relaxed state of mind developed through meditation is the best way to keep oneself from being confused or distracted.

With a guided meditation one can help the dying person to adjust mind again to what is essential. With this, one succeeds in finding space and freedom in one's own consciousness again. There are innumerable practices to align the experiencer with aspects of his nature, without distraction. If the dying persons that one is accompanying are oriented to Buddhism but have not accumulated any meditation experience in life, it is very useful to have the image of the Buddha above their heads, into whose heart they want to go. As an expression of their inner nature, his state is a safe refuge. To the dying ones who are open to it, it is very helpful to guide them accordingly. Again, for the caregiver, the results create more space in mind.

> My terminally ill student Sys and her friends rounded off each evening of her day by invoking the buddhas through their usual meditation. In this way, they remembered the teachings of their teachers and made wishes for all the sick who had more difficult conditions than she had. For all participants, orienting to what is essential was an integral part of the daily routine, and years of habit showed its meaning during those days. Despite all circumstances, they were able to give joy and strength to their surroundings, and they quickly became something special in the hospital. The nursing staff was constantly being asked who those people were and where one could book their caring service. The blessing was obviously noticeable to everyone.

Wisdom

Generosity creates openness and connections, which are solidified by meaningful behavior. Practicing patience, one can preserve and secure them and joyful activity makes everything grow. Meditation provides the necessary distance from difficulties and strengthens the attitude to work for the good of beings. The freedom thus gained will definitely let one live happier and more consciously. Therefore, the Tibetans regard the five above-described paramitas or "liberating actions" as strong legs that can run well, but only reach the goal when the eyes of wisdom—as the sixth point—are added. The eyes in turn can see well, but without legs they get nowhere.

Worldly and conditioned wisdoms are taught at schools and universities. They help both individuals and whole societies to live better and be able to do more for others. In particular, the notions of idealism and the capacities for discernment, which are developed in Western countries, are valuable helpers in searching for one's own experiencer, when used without superstition and connected with human maturity. However beautiful, healthy, and free they may create the world, our benefit from them abruptly ends with death—for they are simply worldly.

The ultimate wisdom is timeless and aims at mind itself. But it only arises through properly guided meditation. In the laboratory of mind one discovers, through absorption, that every phenomenon is composite and impermanent, and therefore "empty" of any lasting nature. After this insight, if one looks for the experiencer of this experience, the hands are even emptier: one finds only space. That which experiences simply does not have any material characteristics: not size, width, weight, nor color or taste. But before one signs up for a course in nihilism or dialectical materialism, perhaps one last observation: the experience happens!

If something experiences what is obviously not a thing, the experiencer also cannot disappear. So one is timeless and indestructible, and rather leaves while celebrating life fearlessly and being beneficial for others.

What the world needs—on both the large and small scale—is strong, forward-looking functioning without disturbing emotions. One manages this with certainty if one forgets that, in supporting the dying person, one does something for him—and rather recognizes the inseparability of the totality. This is a huge step toward becoming an adult. The wisdom begins to unfold because a package of selflessness, good wishes, patience, strength, knowledge, skill and a stable mind is used compassionately for someone. When one is confronted with the decay of a body, one can recognize that nothing is "in itself" and yet everything appears—that is the highest teaching!

DYING AS A PROCESS

Knowledge of the inner processes in body and mind is as helpful for one's own preparation for death as it is for people who care for others who are dying. If one knows what to expect while dying, the conditions can be used and fears specifically removed.

The dissolution of the corporeal elements can happen suddenly in an accident, or, because of disease, may also take days, weeks or months. Without the addition of painkillers, the process of dying, when viewed from the outside, looks like this:

When, as described in detail in the previous chapter, the earth element dissolves into the water element, it brings about a slowdown of movements until, in the end, the body can only lie down; without supportive pillows upright sitting is no longer possible. If a dying person asks to be held at this time, physical contact is pleasant and reassuring. The eye-consciousness also decreases and perceptions become unclear.

If one is told from time to time where one is and what exactly is happening, this creates the missing and relieving framework. A time of openness will arise, because games do not work anymore and inner confusion increases. Here one wants to be reminded of successes in life, even those that one made possible for others, but the friends must under no circumstances give hope that everything will be all right again. This is often the last opportunity to consciously say goodbye to one's beloved, friend, or family member and to express one's gratitude; and one should use this opportunity.

On a physical level significant changes become visible now: movements are getting increasingly more random, the limbs cooler and less sensitive, and the eyes are very often more low-lying, too. All of these are signs that the energy has largely withdrawn from the extremities into the center of the body. The withdrawal of the energies toward the central energy channel during dying, unlike what happens in deep sleep, is irreversible and final.

When the water element dissolves into the fire element, the person who is dying has an increased feeling of thirst. If he drinks, however, he doesn't feel any relief.

As mentioned earlier, those who are dying often start to argue and get angry, even right before death. The main reason is that they are neither able to hear correctly nor speak intelligibly. The intellect loses more and more clarity. The mantras of the Buddha of Limitless Light **OM AMI DEWA HRIH** or of Loving Eyes **OM MANI PEME HUNG** help the dying person as well as the caregiver to raise everything to a beyond-personal level.

The energies then continue to pull back toward the heart center, while the consciousness dwells in the body axis between the top of the head and the power center below the navel. As an observer, one can no longer assume that one still is understood correctly by the dying person.

The fire element now dissolves into the air element, and the dying person loses control of the heat. He feels cold and wants to be covered with warm blankets, but they cannot compensate for the loss of inner heat. The last heat is experienced in the heart center. After that, breathing becomes more unsteady, one loses control, and breathing gets increasingly difficult—the so-called death-rattle.

Now the wind element starts to dissolve into the space element. According to the old descriptions, the dying person who is not using painkillers behaves like a drowning man, gasping wildly for air. Fear can increase immensely here, and everyone knows that things are coming to an end.

Even someone who has meditated a lot and is already looking forward to seeing the buddhas whose closeness one feels more and more, can rarely prevent the body from fighting once again and rising up. After all, it is its task to survive.

Here the last connections to this life tear, but those to the beloved still hold. In countless examples it is reported that someone was only able to die when the close friend left the room. Now loved ones, therefore, can influence the dying process through their presence or absence while the dying one switches between states of being awake and deep unconsciousness. The last moments are filled with three long breathings-out without breathing in again, after which the dying person is generally found to be dead.

For confirmation of death, medical practice still waits until there is no more electrical activity measured in the cells of the brain stem due to lack of oxygen.

As described in the previous chapter, from a Buddhist point of view the onset of death has not happened yet; the wind has merely completely dissolved into the space element. Relatives or caregivers should have already arranged with doctors and nurses in advance, so that they can spend an hour quietly with the body without its being touched. Thus, the inner processes are not disturbed until the final death.

Instructions from *The Tibetan Book of the Dead*[22]

To recognize the Clear Light that appears during dying.

Listen, (name)!
In this moment you should see a path. As soon as you stop breathing, you see the primordial, radiant light. This is the first phase of dying, which your teacher has explained to you during your life. It is the true reality, empty and unadorned as space. This is your primordial mind, untainted and unadorned, without center and without limits, empty and radiant. Recognize this state as what it is, and step into it! If this point is reached, I'll help you to recognize it.

The caregiver whispers these words again and again into the ear of the dying one, in order to imprint them on him, until the visible outer breathing ceases. Just before the breathing stops, the caregiver turns the dying person on his side, in such a way that he adopts the posture of a *sleeping lion*. Along with this, he reads the text so that the dying person knows what follows. At this moment all beings experience the true reality that is without mistake. This is the first phase of dying, the radiant light of reality.

SPECIAL CHALLENGES

Dealing with Pain

In Western industrialized countries, one has the good karma to rarely have to suffer severely on the physical level, because proper help is fortunately ensured by the system and the right painkillers are available everywhere and are prescribed at the appropriate time.

It is a commonly held idea that more suffering at the end of life means more "purification" and that one could still get rid of a lot of negative impressions, which will then no longer accompany one into the next life. But this is not the case. Negative impressions are already used up at the moment of their appearance. The moment the snake has bitten, they are already dissolved. From that point it is just a matter of moderating the consequences. Doing nothing effective against the karmic result of disease—the pain—is a mistake that brings no merit. One purifies neither more nor less by enduring unnecessary suffering. Rather it weakens the willpower for the next life, if one allows the state to expand. It is much more mature and wise to take advantage, without drama, of all the possibilities of help and to adjust oneself to the fundamentally inherent abilities such as fearlessness, joy, strength and love. This stores much better impressions in consciousness for the future life.

Assisted Suicide

Assisted suicide is a difficult matter and touches both the karma and the attitude of those involved. In Buddhism it is generally advised against since seventy-two thousand buddha energies, inherent in the body, are deliberately destroyed through that. Whoever, out of compassion, helps someone who is suffering severely to kill himself, acts mostly unwittingly and therefore harvests few negative impressions. But whoever assists in a suicide must deal with the fact that everything painful that was now avoided waits anew for the dying person in the next life. Already the image of a similar future is usually sufficient to refrain from doing that. Also, consciously killing oneself, especially when painkillers are available and if one does not act in complete panic, creates similar habits for future lives.

What happens to people who are connected to a life support machine without any other vital signs? Usually the family decides. The general advice here would be, if one has decided to switch it off, do so at the new moon or full moon because these are the times when the energies of the two side channels of the body move into the central channel. This creates the best conditions for the following intermediate states and for a good rebirth. The mind is clearer on these days and, with good stored impressions, the stream of experience can easily move up and exit through one of the upper orifices. This should ease the dying process.

In most cases assisted suicide comes into question when the doctors have given up and a cure is hopeless or when the process of dying has irreversibly begun. By causing the premature death, a doctor accelerates or facilitates the dying. What killing exactly means is established and appraised quite differently across jurisdictions around the world. Using the example of Socrates, it becomes clear how crucial the perspective is here:

One day Socrates (468–399 BC and about the same time as Buddha) was sitting on a wall at the edge of a market square when a man stormed past him, followed shortly by an angry horde of club-wielding men. These screamed at Socrates: "Grab him, he is a murderer!" "Ah, he's a butcher." "No," one replied hastily, "he has killed a human being!" Socrates then said calmly: "Oh, he is a soldier." The mob, already real Greeks at that time, meanwhile paused in puzzlement and then responded, "No, no, he has killed a man on purpose!" "Yes, then I understand," smiled Socrates, "he must be an executioner." Meanwhile, the fleeing man had already disappeared into the alleys. The pursuers stayed back, confused, as Socrates stood up and walked away.

Even in Buddhism, killing, which of course creates a lot of suffering in general, can be evaluated from a broader context. In one of his last five hundred lives before enlightenment, Buddha himself killed a man who was about to kill five hundred others. On the one hand, he did that to save the man from further negative actions and thus protect him from a very difficult karma; on the other hand, he did it to save many other lives. According to the economic instinct, it was the right thing to do and was beneficial for everyone except for himself.

In the case of assisted suicide, which some countries allow their citizens to choose, a vast field of outer and inner conditions comes together and one can only advise not to cherish selfish wishes.[23] But this does not protect against sinister characters, who like to see themselves as rulers over life and death, as is sometimes the case in nursing homes. One can probably act really healthily and altruistically only when there is a mature humaneness and no deficiency. A few years ago in Moscow I represented Buddhist knowledge on a television show on this subject. All the members of the panel agreed as a matter of course that assisted suicide should not be permitted in Russia; because of the housing shortage in the country, doctors would actually already be bribed to perform assisted suicide, only to get a coveted apartment. It would then only be a matter of time before family members would be tempted to do the same with aging or sick relatives.

Organ Donation

Every year in the United States over 22,000 people get organ transplants, harvested from a little over 8,000 human bodies.[24] The heart, heart valves, liver, lung, and blood vessels can be removed from the dead, as well as auditory ossicles, corneas, bone tissue, tendons, and the cerebral membrane. Seen this way, the human being is a giant warehouse of spare parts and everybody is a potential donor or recipient of a vital organ. The condition for organ donation is the unambiguous determination of brain death, because only then does the harvesting begin, with the respective approval for organ donation. Organ donation is one of the major controversial issues of contemporary medicine, in part because the fast developments in the field of medical technology make possible a handling of the human being and his body that eliminates both the systems that have been taken for granted in this regard and the former boundaries between life and death.

From a Buddhist perspective, it is very useful to have in one's possession an organ donor card, so that, in case of an early death, one can give others a better or longer life with one's healthy organs. But if one feels uncomfortable with this idea, one should not feel any pressure or one should opt for a tissue donation, since tissue can basically be removed even up to seventy-two hours after biological death.[25] Everyone can and should die as he wants and, if one is able to extend the life of others through one's own death, that is generous. But just as meaningful is the wish to go through the dying process consciously and undisturbed, in order to reach liberation through the learned meditations. Helping all beings from this level of consciousness is immeasurable.

The fact that there are courageous and compassionate people willing to give away their body after death for the benefit of others is great and praiseworthy. One also obtains a final push of good karma for one's further path. According to both Buddha's teachings and the insights of near-death research, though, there are some notable additions and spiritual attitudes: If possible, the spiritual teacher of the deceased should support the process in order to avoid shocks and also to build up the good impressions that such a donor deserves.

If this can be done in the right way, an organ donation would be the ultimate realization of the practice of *Chöd*—the practice of "cutting through"—of Tibetan accomplishers. In meditation, one here reaches complete freedom, by imagining the giving away of one's own body to hungry beings that one nourishes, and along with it dissolves all attachment to "oneself." If prepared in this way, mind can joyfully use the possibilities of the intermediate state and go where this attitude of mind leads it, for the good of all beings.

While the energies are coming together after the cardiac arrest, the awareness of the donor still remains highly conscious in space. Therefore, I could imagine the ideal process of an organ donation in the West for Buddhists, Christians and other well-meaning people in such a way: Since the body has to be opened before cardiac death for medical reasons, it is advisable to act with the highest empathy possible. Only after thirty minutes from the onset of death from a Buddhist perspective—when either the

heart has been removed or a cardiac arrest has occurred—is
the dead person completely unaware.

Since the brain-dead person therefore experiences what
happens in the operating room, how his body is treated, and
how the staff speaks about him, and also clearly feels the
attitude of those present, all those involved should keep the
noble donor continually in mind. The best is if his trusted
Buddhist teacher, a friend, or a mature family member—or an
already prepared audio-device—explains to him the vast value
of his gift, how entire families will become happy through this,
and how the unlimited kindness of his action enriches himself.
During the surgery this person or the doctor should explain in
their mind the meaning of the processes to the dying person.
After the organs are harvested and thus other lives could be
prolonged, at the end one can tell him: "Now you are really
free, you did the best for these beings. Go now to the clearest
light or the finest parents who attract you, and keep on working
for beings. Your noble example will be celebrated!"

It is questionable to what extent the consciousness, as
already described, not only withdraws into the heart center
during dying but also still retains its connection there. In
the late 1990s the internationally recognized Christian
neuropsychologist Dr. Paul Pearsall published a sensational
book, *The Heart's Code*, with amazing reports of seemingly
inexplicable changes in taste, behavior, memories, and habits of
those receiving transplanted hearts.[26] According to his research,
these changes in the organ recipients strongly correspond to
the personality characteristics of the organ donors.

Recent studies point out, however, that other cell complexes
—such as lung, liver, and kidneys—also store memories, habits

and preferences of people and that therefore, no personal mind, which is actually a stream of impressions, finds a new home with the heart of the deceased. The attitudes and habits of the recipient are added to the transplantation data stored in the cells. Depending on how open the recipient is toward them, these influences are perceived and adopted in different degrees. Under all circumstances, the one who is blessed with an organ should think of the donor with much gratitude and make wishes that he himself could do a similar thing for others one day.

Suicide

Suicide is basically a bad idea and, above all, offers no long-term solution. Except under very special circumstances, it is the most harmful thing that one can do to oneself because it leaves more impressions full of suffering in the mind than a stranger's murder. From a Buddhist perspective, one can only advise against it because suicide creates a habit of doing it again in future lives. This also explains why many suicidal people are "love struck" with this thought and often, in spite of caring attempts by relatives and friends, or many hours of therapy, simply cannot let go of the idea any more. With every suicide the outlook for future favorable living conditions worsens, because one goes directly against one's own buddha nature. The seventy-two thousand energy channels in the body contain buddha energies, which one destroys by one's own hand. Accordingly, apart from killing a Buddhist teacher or one's own parents, suicide is considered one of the most grievous negative actions.

Whoever thinks about killing oneself should be aware that life will be deeply painful in the next rebirth. One can be sure to find oneself under difficult conditions such as finding oneself again in uncivilized regions of the world (e.g. certain parts of Africa). This explanation is certainly not a psychological trick or racist joke. The conditions in most places of the big southern continent, the way people treat one another, and the diseases and oppressions that they are suffering, correspond quite precisely to Buddha's descriptions of the karmic effects of suicide.

Unfortunately, too many think the self-created end of their lives would also end their suffering. Or they even hope that, by killing infidels along with their suicide, they will earn a place close to their god. Whatever the individual triggers are, Buddha named three basic causes and their effects:

Stupidity: the belief that, after the destruction of the body, pain and despair would be over. This is of course an error, since mind, because unborn and not made up of parts, also cannot be killed. Therefore everything unfinished follows one into the next life. In severe cases the effect of this act leads to a rebirth with fur and four paws.[27]

Attachment: the assumption of not being able to live anymore without someone. The thought easily emerges if a close partner dies or one was abandoned. One doesn't want to live without the beloved one anymore. In the worst case, this action leads to a rebirth as a hungry ghost.

Anger: the idea of disturbing or hurting others. There is often a thought of revenge behind it: "I'll show you what you've done to me!" or "You'll see how you'll get along without me!" Buddha considers anger to be the most serious cause of suicide. Anger may lead to paranoia states in the hell realm and must be avoided at all costs.

To kill oneself doesn't solve any problems; on the contrary; one only postpones them until the next life under considerably more difficult circumstances.

HELP BEYOND DEATH

For everyone who dies there is still the possibility to have an impact on the mind over the seven weeks following death. Despite the lack of sensory impressions, the misconception of being an "I," separated from the totality, still persists.

As long as the ripening karma of the deceased has not yet led to a new rebirth, it is possible to do good actions in his name or to send wishes for a most pleasant intermediate state and a good new life. Since space doesn't have any limitations, wishes will also reach their goal. One can strengthen this attitude again with the mantras **OM AMI DEWA HRIH** or **OM MANI PEME HUNG**, which align everything to the state of highest joy.

As the consciousness of the deceased likes to visit places and people that had a strong influence on his life, it is wise to think and speak only favorably about him and to leave his favorite places or cherished possessions untouched, if possible, for up to forty-nine days after death. If the deceased was generous and already gave away and donated part of his fortune while still alive, one should, however, fulfill this wish as soon as possible. In this way his mind receives additional good karma for the intermediate state and his rebirth. After seven weeks, the deceased has arrived in a new life and the heirs can argue or send dozens of lawyers without disturbing him in his development.

Another, already also in the West well-kown method for the loved ones during the intermediate state is the reading of Buddhist texts, which give direction and advice to the dead.

This stream of good wishes and actions is the best support for the dead, as is the main message of *The Tibetan Book of the Dead:* "Do not fear, everything is your own mind!" When one thinks of the deceased during the seven weeks, one can repeat it quickly. If this sentence is fully understood in a bodiless state, it can lead to liberation. Already in the process of dying such teachings provide space, even though one is so busy with the physical decline. But, if they show up in mind when awakening afterward, they are striking. Thus one has a real advantage afterward, when one is without any physical distractions and with high intelligence. *The Tibetan Book of the Dead* mentions that one is nine times more talented without the blocked energy channels of a non-yogic body than in the current situation—and has huge benefit from such wisdoms. With this support, the deceased can either experience liberation from cyclic existence on the levels of joy or even truth, or just use the good impressions for a rebirth for the benefit of many.

Funeral and Mourning Ceremony

In Tibet funerals were different, depending on the deceased person. One usually laid the dead on the bier at home for the first three to five days. In the three "old" lineages, one invited accomplishers or hired monks, who read aloud out of *The Tibetan Book of the Dead* on important days during the seven weeks after dying.

The funeral afterward corresponded, if possible, to the prevailing element of his year of birth in order to bring the body back into the best possible accordance with the cycle of becoming and decaying.

If one was born into an earth year according to the Kalachakra calendar, one was buried; in the water year, put into a river; and, in a fire year, burnt, if there was enough wood.

Still today the air burial is used the most because it also gives the deceased a boost of good karma on the path. Before sunrise the body is taken to the site for dismembering and fed to vultures, who are, however, often too big to be able to fly particularly high. They are huge and when they fly over one's head, one has slanting shoulders and a center parting of the hair afterward. The Tibetans like to see them as bodhisattvas that give the dead a last blessing.

Morticians (Skt. Ragyapas) dismember and feed the corpse to vultures within the frame of the air burial. [28]

Cremation was used mostly for middle-ranking lamas. For many centuries, in the case of very highly realized lamas, a stupa was built around them, filled with the physical remains or ashes of the deceased, and people took blessing from it.

What happens to the body of the dead is ultimately important only for the bereaved. Nowadays, there are numerous opportunities for a funeral: from cremation and urn burial at the cemetery to burial in a space-balloon or in the sea, and even to being pressed into a diamond. It helps in the decision if the deceased has previously expressed his wishes about how to deal with the body.

The funeral itself is a conscious farewell. In the speech at the grave, one should speak according to the feelings of those present and their education, mentioning the continuing of life, the general and beyond-personal dimension of impermanence. If one informs those present that the deceased has moved from a place where he was vulnerable into a protected state and now lives on in the experience of all, they will look into the future with a more relaxed feeling. If those present are open to it, one can also say something about rebirth and perhaps the nature of mind. One ends with good memories of the dead, sends him good wishes, and eventually gives everyone a minute to thank the deceased. The idea that the deceased has now entered a blissful state, that he is now glad about those present, or that he may soon come back with a lot of surplus will help everybody.

From a Buddhist understanding one should celebrate and honor the dead. A loving, affirmative taking leave of the deceased is the greatest gift one can give him and the family. In this way, one gives him or her the best possible boost for further development and plants good impressions into the mind-stream. A clinging and desperate attitude like "I miss you!" or "Why have you left me?" doesn't help anybody and is unpleasant for the dead one because, however much he would also like it, there is no way back. Because people will see one another again and the deceased will feel well anyway, mourning from a Buddhist point of view is pure attachment and unnecessary, but of course very understandable from a simple human perspective. Just as in the past with the Teutons—and as is still widespread today in Scandinavia and Ireland—one highlights the achievements of the dead in such a celebration. Three or four days after the passing away, when from a Buddhist perspective the consciousness of the deceased awakens from the shock of dying, all his friends come together, have a party, and tell one another all the exciting experiences that they shared with the deceased.

Mourning

Buddhists learn early that every conditioned happiness is impermanent and that every relationship ends with death. Therefore, together they try to orient themselves to lasting values and at the same time to enjoy the good times. Every encounter becomes precious with this attitude, because it could have also been the last. For those who meditate, impermanence is a constant companion and each practice leads to thoughts about the preciousness of this life and then to impermanence: one cannot hold on to anything and should therefore, by all means, use the moment now.

Even if one assumes that the deceased is not suffering anymore, for many it is not easy to apply the teachings right away and let the feeling of loss pass by. Buddhists often try not to mourn loudly during the first forty-nine days, in order not to disturb the beloved in his further development. But the teachings that all the good that one has shared will bring one together with another joyfully in the next life very rarely help.

From a Buddhist point of view, grief is a very strong, painful and captivating emotion. The mourning period forms the natural transition into the next phase of life without the deceased. It takes a relatively long time for habits to be dissolved and new connections to be built up. Actually, from early childhood onward, all of life is shaped by letting go, coming and going; but with the loss of a loved person, it becomes exceedingly obvious. This period, therefore, also offers an opportunity to understand many things in one's life, to recognize one's own wishes, and to use the power of emotions for others.

Grieving Mother

A woman whose son had just died had been sent to Buddha because people thought that he knew a medicine that could bring the child back to life again. Buddha promised his help and asked the woman to pick up mustard seeds from a house where no one had yet died. Despite a thorough search, she found no such house; everywhere parents, spouses, grandparents or children had already died. When Buddha asked for the mustard seeds after her return, she was not able to give him any. Buddha then told her that whatever would be born had to die at one point, sooner or later. Only one thing would be really reliable and lasting, namely one's own mind, our buddha nature.

Meditation is particularly helpful in this phase of life. It reminds one again and again of the dreamlike character of all phenomena and the lightness of being. Open retreats can help to cope with the new situation, and friends in Buddhist centers happily support the transition. For Buddhists, it is particularly important to meet the teacher in this time. He will, like Buddha in the meeting with the grieving woman who has lost her child, point out a beyond-personal view that gives mind more space to handle the loss. Along with that, he can help figure out ways to shape the new life and use it meaningfully. Through his assurance, confidence and power grow.

Everybody goes through four stages of mourning, more or less: First one freezes up, doesn't want to allow the feeling, and consciously works against it. Then, feelings of loss appear and one looks for explanations. After a long period of solitude, one opens up again more intensely to the environment. Afterward, one is able to hold the lost one in his heart and, at the same time, enjoy life again.

In whatever stage one currently is, it is important to understand that dying, death, and loss happen to everybody, so it is not personal. During the mourning period it is wise to use as much of the power of emotions as possible in other fields, while one continues to work inwardly with one's experience and with it also helps others in the same situation.

If you ask Tibetan lamas for antidotes, they will certainly offer compassion, but simultaneously affirm that every grief happens only on the basis of attachment.

Marpa

After the death of his son Tarma Dode, a student asked the great accomplisher Marpa (1012–1097), who brought the Kagyü lineage to Tibet: "How are you?" Marpa replied, "Miserable."

The man was stunned. He asked, "Miserable?" But Marpa laughed. He said, "Yes, but with a difference, and the difference is that the misery is voluntary. Sometimes, in order to have a taste of the world, I move out into it, but I stay the master at the same time. At any moment I can go back inside, and it makes sense to move within the opposites. Then one stays alive." Marpa added, "Sometimes I move into the grief, but grief is nothing that happens to me. I see it and stay untouched."

THE CRUCIAL MOMENT

When the white and the red light come together, twenty to thirty minutes after cardiac arrest, thirty-three feelings of anger and forty feelings of attachment have returned into space. Now the seven emotions that arise out of stupidity dissolve. Beyond all impressions and experiences, all ideas and perceptions then finally disappear. Everything gets dark and quiet. This is the last moment in the bardo of dying.

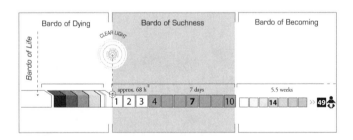

Bardo of death in a chronological overview

THE CLEAR LIGHT OF THE TRUTH STATE

Now the overwhelming radiance inherent in mind breaks through in a flash. This is the crucial moment that one can already focus on and look forward to during one's lifetime, if one works with one's mind. Now, after all sensory impressions, expectations, and mixed emotions have dissolved, there is only one thing left: the experiencer itself, that which has always been sought after. It is never so directly "itself" as it is here. "It is a non-created, natural, non-artificial state of mind in which there is no arising, existing and passing away."[29] As a meditator one tries to approach one's own timeless nature in each state of absorption, but usually remains trapped and influenced by changing experiences. Only after years of practice can the state be experienced that one simply gets as a gift in death. Whoever is able to hold it, hold out in it, and extend it into time and space, becomes a buddha himself. Just as a fish jumps out of the water, mind is free now, playful, and limitless. With the cessation of all binding, obstructing, and limiting effects of past actions and without the separation between the experiencer and the experienced, one experiences mind's timeless essence. Beyond all notion of conscious and unconscious, not bound by any habits, and without distractions of a body, the awareness of the deceased now experiences its boundless luminosity at the heart level.

One dwells in an all-encompassing "aha" experience, similar to when a child in a dark hallway pushes open the door into a light-filled hall. Experiencing, experiencer, and the experienced are fresh, one and true in itself; everything is naked awareness—without any questioning. Insights that emerge in this moment directly connect the experiencer, the world, and the experience in the here and now.

The Tibetans speak of *chönyi bardo*, which when translated from Sanskrit means "the experience of Dharmata." In the

West it is called "the intermediate state of suchness," the radiant-conscious clear light, or the "Truth Space." If this is experienced in the moment of death, it is also called "son-clear light." It is utterly overwhelming in its power and experiences itself as a limitless radiance. Everything that can be experienced or imagined is inherent in the space of naked awareness. If one's own "son-clear light" melts with the "mother-clear light" of the all-pervasive awareness of space, everything is recognized and realized and the state of the Great Seal is reached. The son corresponds to what the deceased experienced of the Clear Light during the melting phase of the meditation. The mother embodies the boundless and ever-present Clear Light, the state of timeless suchness that one meets now. Since one already knows the taste, one will spontaneously melt with it.

From this moment on, one is everything good, meaningful, and protective everywhere. But from this buddha level one no longer appears automatically with recognizable qualities and a body that is graspable by the senses.

Following one's own earlier promises and the wishes of the students, from this highest field of development, but also as a bodhisattva, one can let oneself be reborn in any desired location, work through several bodies at the same time and, above all, appear wherever the beings have a connection to one.

Whether one has chosen at enlightenment to merge completely and limitlessly into conscious space as a blessing or to look again for a body in order to work for the direct benefit of beings, in both cases there is no falling back into the conditioned world. However, the tie of a human body to the senses is connected with a lot of confusion through birth, childhood, and youth over the years, until mind experiences its familiar clarity again through meditation practice.

In Tibet this special relation to one's own body was aptly called "illusory body" (Skt. *nirmanakaya,* Tib. *tulku*), since one experiences not being the body, but having it, and is very aware of the dreamlike character of all phenomena. From this moment on, by example, one opens the hearts of the students eager to learn. When leaving an illusory body— whether used for better or sometimes worse—everyone returns to the beyond-personal pure realms of the buddhas, with the recognition of the Clear Light. When seen in this way, there is no cause for concern that one might lose one's realization while working for the benefit of all in the conditioned world. If emanations act strangely in the world, they unfortunately can only do less for beings in later incarnations.

Consciously dwelling in the Clear Light, therefore, brings forth an unshakeable, boundless realization. This state of inseparability of all phenomena corresponds to the Truth State *(Dharmakaya)* of mind. The path there is appropriately called "Phowa into the Truth State" (see Fig. Conscious Dying).

Meditation masters use the moment of death to call attention to the possibilities of mind. Their art of controlling it is meant to awaken trust. I know three possibilities of how one can connect as a meditator to the Clear Light of the Truth State in the bardo of suchness:

- One simply breathes out the consciousness, and timeless space meets outside and inside, as Kalu Rinpoche and Dilgo Khyentse Rinpoche showed in their deaths (see "The Art of Dying"). Just as the inside of the jar of Manibhadra, by breaking, became one with the surroundings, so too death offers the opportunity by becoming one to experience the fundamental truth of all life: like space, the essence of mind remains untouched by change and death.[30]

- Another form is the longer dwelling of the mind in a state of suchness in the heart of the deceased. It is called *tudam* in Tibetan. Here, as long as the mind doesn't break away from it, the body stays warm and smooth and slowly gets ever smaller.[31] It is said that the length of time one stays in this state depends on the wishes made during one's lifetime. During this time, the mind goes through all the necessary stages of development until enlightenment.

- A third possibility is, with the help of a very difficult meditation that is applicable only in complete solitude, transforming the vibrations of the solid body into energy. In Tibetan it is called *djalu*, which means "rainbow body." Here only hair, nails, and teeth of the dead remain, which—hardly surprisingly—are revered as relics. I personally know of only one person from my years in the Himalayas who realized this: Karmapa's silversmith from Rumtek.[32] Unfortunately, this Phowa of the absolute highest realization is currently dying out in Tibet, because the results do not agree much at all with the dialectical materialism of the Chinese Communists. Earlier, even the families of the yogis who realized this practice were killed.

Depending on the sharpness of mind and direction of the stored karmic impressions, at the end of each life the Clear Light of the Truth State offers to the dying a flash-like experience of enlightenment, which should be held. The best preparation for this moment is having confidence in the teaching and practicing the melting phase in daily meditation. If one succeeds in dwelling in the naked awareness of the experiencer and simply being "the perception itself," undisturbed by mixed feelings, expectations, or sensory impressions, this is a first-class preparation for extending the arising Clear Light into the boundless, twenty to thirty minutes after the last breathing-out. Devotion and trust in enlightenment here give power, and whoever can stand for himself, because he thought, said, and also did the same thing and matured beyond-personally through love, has the opportunity in the intermediate state to realize the true nature of mind and ultimately to dwell in the so-called Truth State of mind.

But if one has meditated little or half-heartedly in life and has had little desire for the melting phase, the depth of the insight gained is not enough to reach enlightenment in the intermediate state. The Clear Light appears in death even for the smallest fly, but the ability to experience it and to consciously dwell in the here and now is the result of responsible honesty, brave intentions, regular practice, and wishes for enlightenment in this lifetime for the benefit of others. Whoever lived with little consciousness, then experiences only a terrifying flash of one's inherent wisdom after the darkness. Living without conviction and other kinds of cowardice are hereby fundamental obstacles for any realization, as is the tendency to hide from unpleasant facts or to leave the problems to the offspring. Being a bleeding-heart who does not want to see and disregarding as well as clinging to obviously outdated and harmful views, leaves behind difficult habits in mind.

In short, the experience of the timeless Clear Light is often so unfamiliar and powerful for non-meditators that they cannot stand it. If in death one backs off from the automatically enlightened vastness of space and its radiance, a deep unconsciousness, similar to a huge wave, crashes over one.

THE LIGHT FORMS OF THE JOY STATE

If one has not been able to hold the Clear Light, this uncon-sciousness lasts about three days; many texts say seventy-two or more hours. According to my experience it is about sixty-eight hours for educated people. Then mind, after deep unconsciousness, comes around again, either abruptly or as out of a deep sleep.

One is still in the intermediate state of the ultimate nature, is still without an "I"-perception, and now gets a second chance to recognize one's mind on a beyond-personal and liberating level through the melting with a familiar buddha form, and to thus liberate oneself.

Unaffected by ideas of a self, a body or its sensory impressions, everything appears on the highest level of pure form. All beings are then buddhas, as one has always imagined it after the melting phase in meditation. All sounds are mantras, and all thoughts self-arisen direct wisdom. This state usually lasts one week—that means from the third to

the tenth day—and expresses the playful Joy State of mind
(Skt. *sambhogakaya,* Tib. *longku*) between the Truth State
(Skt. *dharmakaya,* Tib. *chöku*) that was missed in death and
the powerful Emanation State (Skt. *nirmanakaya,* Tib. *tulku*)
that will appear later. The beyond-personal three states are
also forms of expression of the ultimate State of Essence (Skt.
svabhavikakaya, Tib. *ngowonyiku*), just as humidity, clouds,
rain, and snow are all forms of water.

Four Buddha States *				
English	Truth State	Joy State	Emanation State	Essence State
Sanskrit	dharmakaya	sambhogakaya	nirmanakaya	svabhavikakaya
Tibetan	chöku	longku	tulku	ngowonyiku
realization	fearlessness	joy	love	equanimity
view	timeless space	playful multiplicity	limitlessness	oneness of all phenomena
experience	direct insight	self-arisen joy	meaningful action	effortless dwelling
comparison	water vapor	clouds	rain	water
* see extended explanations: Nydahl, O.: The Great Seal, 2007				

In this second part of the bardo of suchness the mind
dwells in its richness of pure phenomena. One experiences the
enlightening buddha forms and their power-fields, but only if
one has developed a relationship to them in past lives through
blessing, transmission, guided meditations, and empowerments
and if the building-up phase of the meditation (in which one

adjusts to its light-energy forms) was practiced well. It is like a sky full of radiant light. Some see moving lights or spots of light there; others experience a buddha or even a hundred buddha forms.

The teachings described here were given by Buddha to his closest students. Over the centuries they were passed on in India, often orally, and the accuracy of the transmission was confirmed again and again through the state of absorption and the memory of the respective transmission holders. In Tibet these were enlightened accomplishers like Guru Rinpoche, Marpa and the Karmapas.

There were two transmissions from India. The old tantras[33] (i.e. the secret teachings of Buddha encompassing body, speech, and mind) reached Tibet around the year 750 through Guru Rinpoche in a form equipped with many details. They include the bardo texts, translated and explained in many languages, and very precisely describe the process of the individual impressions and experiences in this intermediate state, as well as the possibilities for those who received a special Buddhist empowerment called *shitro*.[34] Through this empowerment, the subconscious appears in the intermediate state of the ultimate nature as one hundred different buddhas: forty-two peaceful forms then condense out of the energy center at the heart level and fifty-eight critically protective ones from the head center.

In the new tantras, which came to Tibet with Marpa and the second Buddhist wave around 1050, however, the peaceful and protecting forms are not described at all because, in fact, only those who are highly realized can hold such pictorial experiences. Since they are often portrayed in magnificent painted thangkas, and in the books of many of my teachers and colleagues, I will not expand on them in detail.

It is more important that one meditates on a particular buddha form during life, repeats his mantra, and enjoys the building-up phase. In the intermediate state of suchness this buddha form will manifest as a self-arisen expression of mind. One doesn't have to imagine it anymore. It is the directly shining experience (the Clear Light of the Joy State). If one has recognized it, one melts with it and thus gains liberation. This process is also called *Phowa into the Joy State.* Then one no longer has to live through the intermediate state of becoming and experiences the fruits of one's meditation.

Here one's own buddha nature appears unveiled in all its richness and without attachment to an imagined "I," bringing all levels of space and appearance together in a fulfilling way. It testifies to the unity of experiencer, experience, and the experienced, shows itself always anew, and makes the blessing of an all-encompassing outer and inner view of the world come alive. People who have not trained their minds and have developed little awareness "toward the inner," do not even notice this second part of the bardo of suchness, or only in flash-like, emerging moments of bright colors, dazzling lights, sharp sounds, and terrifying shapes. Everything is so radiant and loud that one cannot stand the intensity, turns away from it in fear, or becomes unconscious again after a very short time.

*The 42 peaceful and 58 protecting buddha forms
in the bardo of suchness (Tib. shitro)*

REBIRTH

The renewed awakening about ten days after death opens up the beginning of a new intermediate state and the path to a worldly rebirth.[35] Here the tendencies and wrong ideas from the past life conquer and cover over the now naked mind again. Now it depends on which impressions one has collected in the past life in one's store-consciousness and, above all, whether one has honestly stood by one's convictions. It is also important how well one has learned to let experiences pass by and to see them as beyond-personal. These conditions—and, in very fortunate cases, the blessing and the attention of a lama—decide whether good states, rather dull experiences, or the beginning of severe suffering are experienced now.

Therefore, whoever did not immediately go from a human life into the power-field of a Buddha in this phase gets to know fields of experiences whose raw material was accumulated mainly during the preceding life.

If one is not aware of this and has not learned to control one's mind, now the confusion of dying continues. Because of the habitual attachment to world and body, one does not want to acknowledge one's passing away and tries not to deal with this fact, if at all possible. Even if one is still lying in the wrecked car because no one could recover the body, or if one decays alone in the apartment, the mind leaves the body and does not look back. Above all, in a sudden death, the insight that one has died is deeply hidden under the firm idea of life and other impressions. The habits that have been built up over countless lives are so strong that at first they simply continue in the bardo of becoming.

Because of the lack of new sensory experiences, the impressions stored in mind unfold and convey to the dead one the impression of his former body in a somewhat familiar setting. The more one is trapped in one's old notions, the more time one needs before realizing that the impressions of the surrounding world and of one's own body are illusory and are based on nothing. Similar to how one experiences the world in a dream—as existing but, at the same time, as something different—even after death one believes the appearing world to be real.

The days after waking up are very animated. One of course leaves one's corpse without looking back and follows one's old habits, but the wish to find out what has happened comes up more and more. Thus one tries more often to meet relatives and friends, to visit familiar places, or to go to work. Since the sensory impressions have disappeared with the body, one experiences the world through vibration and inspiration, and everything appears like on a hazy afternoon or engulfed in fog. Beings and places emerge out of a nebulous surrounding and dissolve into it again. Without the distraction of a body, all levels of insight are available. That is why one is highly talented and perceptive, or even clear-sighted. One is able to perceive beings comprehensively, understand all languages, and read thoughts. One is astonished to the highest degree when one perceives what close friends actually think about one and how so-called enemies can surprisingly keep one in mind in a friendly way. Without a body, the mind condenses everywhere, wherever its thoughts direct it, and all feelings and emotions are experienced directly and very strongly.

If one has not built up the habit in life of keeping one's mind relaxed and, through meditation, in one place, and generally thinks that the impressions are real, one lives through these days as a big mess. One is driven back and forth by one's own confused thoughts, memories and feelings. Countless pictures collide constantly, depending on the habits one has formed in life and the thoughts one had while dying. The mental confusion has exactly the same emotional tone as in the last life. But at some point, when one yet again goes through a door without having opened it, walks on sand without leaving footprints, looks into the mirror and no reflection appears, or when one dips his hand in boiling water and it doesn't hurt—one knows beyond a doubt: "I am dead."

For a short while, one is very confused about this. Some teachers speak of a very short return to unconsciousness, from which one wakes up immediately. Now one increasingly loses the connection to the past life. At first, mind still fluctuates between the familiar world of experience of the past life and the increasingly emerging tendencies and feelings from the store-consciousness. But then the collected impressions of all lives take the lead. Depending on whether the stream of emotions in the store consciousness of the deceased is inclusive and warm or calculating and "I"-related, the time in bardo is experienced as pleasant or painful. With either joy or increasing fear, one recognizes that the field of future possibilities narrows more and more. After half of the seven weeks after death, which one can spend in intermediate states between last life and rebirth (meaning after about twenty-five days), the alignment of the stream of consciousness gets clear and the future takes shape. If the circle of friends and family is not generous in the name of the deceased now or one does not have a connection with a blessing-holding Buddhist teacher, one is drawn to one of the six possible mind realms that corresponds to the previous thoughts, words and actions, and finds one's next life there.

REBIRTH IN THE REALMS OF EXISTENCE

The six realms of consciousness into which one can be reborn are often described as worlds in Buddhist terminology, similar to Christianity's actually existing heaven and hell, because they are seen by the person concerned as exceedingly real. Because in Buddhism there are no worlds separated from the experiencer, these are also here states of conditioned consciousness. They are not created by something external, or a higher authority, but are rather the result of the attitudes and actions in previous lives. Thus one can be reborn as a god, demigod, human, animal, hungry ghost, or with paranoia.

Although the classical descriptions of the realms sometimes sound pretty strange, in what follows I use the rather medieval-looking images and terms, as my wife Hannah and I received them from our teacher Kalu Rinpoche in Sonada in the Eastern Himalayas in the winter of 1970–71. On one hand, they convey a cultural image; on the other, they also keep the style of transmission alive. It is good to remember while reading that it is not about the actions of an unpleasant, judging god but about self-generated perceptions and feedback, similar to the unending play of mind in dreams and to experiences of intoxication.

Buddha describes the ranges of unenlightened impressions that are experienced in a human body as the suffering that is caused by birth, sickness, old age, and death. The constant striving for happiness, wanting to avoid pain, clinging to what is pleasant, and having to endure what is unavoidable—all of this keeps the mind occupied. For example, one learns this when passing gorgeous houses, in the gossip stories of the tabloids, in the lives of eager citizens who cannot find permanent values, among fellow humans who seek only the coarsest stimuli in life, in never-ending trials because of greed, and in people who make an enemy of everything in life.

The range of phenomena generated by mind may be perceived most memorably during a visit to the psychiatric ward. In the smallest area one finds the traits and characteristics of the six realms. Depending on the type of impressions, these states encompass the whole emotional field, from bliss through confusion to suffering. Their basic moods are the well-known disturbing emotions: pride and always knowing better, jealousy and resentment, desire and attachment, confusion and dullness, as well as the realms of stinginess and greed and the whole range of aversion, anger, and hatred. At every moment the disturbing emotions not only influence the present life, but also lay seeds for the future ones.

From this standpoint rebirth, too, is not mysterious at all. The mind—like a mirror—simply continues to behave in the same way as it already is doing in this life: if one is sour, one only meets sour people; if happy, one meets happy people. This general secret extends beyond death: tendencies continue and are the cause for future experiences.

Taken together, the six worldly realms are called *samsara* (from Sanskrit, meaning "the coming and going") or *khorwa* ("wheel" in Tibetan) and are depicted in the pictures very vibrantly but neatly arranged as a wheel of life with six fields.

Rebirth in the Three Realms of Suffering

If emotions and harmful actions like hatred, envy, and greed prevail in mind, one is reborn in the three lower realms. Worst of all are the effects of anger, the most difficult of all emotions:

Hell Realms: The World of Hatred

Already in dying, and reinforced during the bardo of becoming, those who were very angry in life, emphasized the mistakes of others, and wished them a lot of harm, experience these feelings again, intensified. Everything that Breughel, Bosch and Dante painted and depicted in their images of hell is maturing in this state, which fortunately is conditioned and impermanent like all other unenlightened experiences. The Tibetans, who lacked a protective welfare state, paint eighteen of these states of suffering in gruesome detail, in order to deter the bad guys. They describe eight hot and eight cold hells, a neighboring hell, and an occasional hell, each one more unpleasant than the previous one.

If, on the other hand, one had very quickly emerging emotions, everything feels cold; one tries to run somewhere where it is warm. There, too, the door suddenly slams shut

The Wheel of Life

and one does not come out again. One has the idea that the heavy feelings that one has in mind color the whole world. And this experience is very painful.

One can also see people in this life who experience states of total paranoia and frustration, who uncontrollably get drunk again and again, go through untraceable pain, or are simply desperately unhappy. Although today in Western countries one is under a physician's care and subdued by medication, there are people with paranoia, who hide continuously, injure themselves and are quite sure that there is poison in their glass of water.

Anger is certainly the most devastating emotion with which one can spoil the beautiful garden of one's mind.

Shariputra

Monks, who were often turned over to monasteries in earliest childhood and afterward only know the miracles of femininity through memories of their mothers, often share a touching story about them. A story of the high teacher Shariputra describes how he freed his difficult mother with Buddha's methods. The lady was not easy to deal with, fighting with all the women living in the neighborhood. Her son Shariputra could not stop her from doing that. In the end he knew only one remedy. He hung a bell above the door of the house and taught his mother to say **OM MANI PEME HUNG** while ringing the bell on her way from one dispute with a neighbor to the next.

When she died and, according to her angry content of mind, found herself in a large cauldron of molten metal with like-minded customers, an employee of the hell realm passed by to stir. As his spoon banged against the cauldron, she remembered the sound of the bell above her door and she recited the mantra. On the strength of its liberating impact, her perception changed immediately, and all found themselves in a god realm.

Hungry Ghosts: The World of Greed

If there was a lot of stinginess and greed stored in the stream of consciousness, the previous life was already strongly marked by disappointment and narrowness. One was dominated by things instead of acquiring freedom through them, and was plagued by such heavy dreams and states of mind that one hardly had any peace.

This painful state leads to the realm of the so-called hungry ghosts, since the many different attachments eventually condense into the core needs of hunger and thirst. No matter what one tries now, one is dominated by the feeling that one is never sated. In the texts the outer obstacles are described as follows: Everything edible becomes fire when one wants to bring it to one's mouth, or giants snatch everything away. Inner ideas make the mouth appear as small as the eye of a needle, while the belly takes on the size of a city. Regardless of how much one swallows, the belly is not full. One never reaches satisfaction.

There are even people among us who are so rich that they waste much of their time keeping an eye on their things, so that nothing is lost, rather than using their wealth meaningfully, enjoying it joyfully, and sharing it. Of course, it is okay to keep things that are needed for the near future or may be more useful later. But, if you feel in this life that too much stinginess, greed, and selfish attachment arise, it is good to give away a few things occasionally.

The signs that one is drifting into this direction in the intermediate state are increasing hunger and thirst.

The Animal Realm: The World of Confusion

Confusion brings little joy after death. Whoever consciously lied during the last life to harm others, always stayed calculating in his opinions, and followed the herding instinct, or only strived for the stupidest and roughest stimuli, without using the possibilities of mind, will after death not be able to cope with the vastness of space and its impressions, which appear as images.

The sign that an animal birth is lurking is a dulling of the perceptions. One gets so many veils that one simply cannot withstand the projections of mind, and the confusion keeps growing. One will try to hide among rocks or bushes and, if there are some mating animals nearby, will make the big mistake of going between them. In this way, the next rebirth will possibly have four legs and a nice fur coat, in summer as well as in winter.

No lengthy considerations are necessary to understand how varied animal suffering is. One only needs to go to the slaughterhouse to see that they are not doing well. In turn, domestic animals pay for their food with their freedom. If one looks underground or in the water, where most animals live, they hardly do anything else other than eat one another. Admittedly, some live quite well, such as dogs in civilized, rich homes. But, even in the golden prison of luxury, animals have the problem that they cannot open the tin with the pâté for themselves.

Rebirth in the Three Realms of Conditioned Happiness

The World of Demigods: The World of Jealousy

If one has done good things during life but developed jealousy with it, the feeling after death condenses as a world of demigods, which is marked by resentment and good karma at the same time. Therefore, in the realm of demigods the beings are beautiful, tall, and wealthy, but suffer from constant war among themselves and against the gods. They lead a dangerous life, for they believe that they die when they are pierced by a weapon. The gods with their higher level of consciousness experience this only when their heads fall off. As always, the cause lies in mind. One is fundamentally dissatisfied and resentful, envies others because of their happiness, and wants to possess it oneself. Despite their joys, for which they owe their good karma, they never come to rest. A sure sign that such a rebirth approaches after death is that one goes to an armory and equips oneself there.

God Realms: The Worlds of Pride

If, after the falling away of the sensory impressions, pride shows itself as the strongest storage of the subconsciousness, it leads to a rebirth in the god realm. In this case, one has a large amount of good, rich impressions in the store-consciousness. As gods, the beings show themselves in unspeakably beautiful bodies, imagined as radiant. They experience themselves as being tall, strong, and healthy. Everything happens easily because they have done much good earlier. They feel very good and believe that they understood everything long ago. But each god still thinks that he may be his own "I" and thus separated from the totality.

The world of gods is divided into three groups. The four levels of *formless gods* enjoy the state of pure abstraction and can rest so long in it that they believe they are eternal; the seventeen levels of the so-called *form gods* experience the highest aesthetic pleasure, experience a surrounding of beautiful art and are beyond any desire; and the six realms of *desire gods* immediately get every wish fulfilled.

It is easily possible to build up a lot of pride in today's Western world with good actions or good wishes. After death, one experiences oneself in a palace and begins to walk through unspeakably beautiful halls. One sees a balcony with a bed, lies down to sleep, wakes up as a god again, and experiences one pleasure after another for a seemingly infinite long time.

But, at some point with the gods, the good impressions are used up. Then the god suddenly gets a bad thought and immediately says, "I don't want to think that." With that, he already has two. Soon enough, he thinks "I have to do something about it," and has already the third. In this way, he loses his level of consciousness. Finally, during a period of seven days, he experiences where and when he will be reborn. He sees how few joys he will have, compared to the time as a god, and dies with a lot of suffering.

Therefore, pride and good actions are desirable because they lead into good realms and god worlds, but they are no real refuge. They don't bring a basic security because in that situation one experiences oneself as being separated from the totality and thus even the most joyful impressions remain impermanent.

Human Existence: The World of Desire
A human birth is obtained if one has at least done some good actions and is governed by what one likes rather than what one doesn't like—when attachment is the most prominent emotion in the store-consciousness. Desire does not only

relate to exciting partners, it may also be the strong wish for success, enjoyment, possessions, or other pleasant sensory experiences.

If desire is strongest, one will feel drawn, during the possible seven weeks in the intermediate state after death, to beings with whom one has a close connection and who owe one eighteen years of their peace of mind. And, unfortunately, in life there is generally no choice: if one has not made the promise to work for the benefit of all, one is attracted equally by good and bad connections. Whether earlier one robbed caravans and accepted a few dead guards or merchants with it, or whether one treated the other badly in the marriage, in the beginning of the encounter one just feels tension.

If there were only good relations between people, one would have only loving parents, grateful children, and nice families and everything would be wonderful. It is not only good actions from previous lifetimes that connect, but also what was painful and what harmed oneself or others has glue and creates attraction. In fact, today's family circumstances clearly show what from before binds the members together. If good behavior matures between them, they experience happiness; if not, they disturb each other. It is usually mixed.

The gender depends on the built-up tendencies and the religions. If women have a weak position, as is often the case in desert regions and around the equator, and are treated very badly by men, they often change sex at rebirth, and in the next round the former husband suffers in a woman's body. In free countries, gender is more a result of the attitude: one becomes a woman if one has developed more intuition, and a man if one has developed more playful characteristics in earlier lives.

What inspires people, lets them become active and is really touching, are life's possibilities to also benefit others. Many primarily selfish and ungrateful people, however, just use up their good karma and unwittingly enter into a downward spiral, which lets future rebirths become far more unpleasant than the present one.

But, the biggest advantage of a human birth is to be able to discover the nature of mind. As a human being, one can acquire the necessary freedoms and opportunities to see the mirror behind the pictures and to become aware of the impermanence and unreality of the constant flow of thoughts, emotions, and physical experiences.

Properly used, and under very fortunate circumstances, this birth contains the best possibilities (among the six realms of existence) for achieving lasting meaning. Compared to the beings who experience themselves as being separated from the totality—whether with solid bodies, as human beings and animals have them, or in states of energy and awareness, as the aforementioned gods, demigods, ghosts and hell beings —a human birth offers a very precious foundation from which to strive for timeless values.

Six Realms

	realms	causes	observation	description
Rebirth in the three realms of suffering	hell realm	hatred, **anger,** emphasizing mistakes of others, wishing others evil	paranoia, frustration, permanent unhappiness	18 hells
	hungry ghosts	**greed,** stinginess, disappointment, narrowness	heavy mental states and dreams, satisfaction is never reached, intense restlessness	unsatiable needs of hunger and thirst
	animals	conscious lying for one's own advantage, being politically correct, dulling of the perception, following the stupidest and coarsest stimuli	unclarity, **confusion,** dullness	lack of self-confidence, following instincts & senses "state of very big dullness" (Marpa)
Rebirth in the three realms of conditioned happiness	gods	**pride,** large amount of good and rich impressions	everything goes easily for them; they are tall, strong and healthy	the three god-realms: formless gods *(enjoy abstraction),* form gods *(experience aesthetic joys),* desire gods *(get every wish fulfilled)*
	jealous gods	have done good things, but developed **jealousy** and envy along with it	resentment, distrust, discontent; they are beautiful, tall and wealthy	constant fight against imaginary threat
	human beings	attraction, **desire**	strong striving for success, enjoyment, possessions, pleasant sensory experiences	possibility to develop and to realize oneself; potential for conscious action

LONG-TERM PREPARATION

How can one now best remove from the store-consciousness the painful impressions which have been accumulated in this or previous lives? After their build-up through ignorance, it is a matter of removing the "fiends." A broad sense toward the inner is a good start: the insight that something is not right. If one finds many mixed emotions, these turn this life gray and hopeless. If one constantly judges other people, then one's friends, jobs and money disappear again and again and way too fast. If one hears oneself continuously complain about what terrible things happen to oneself, these are indications of a possible decline. These are clear signs that a situation has been reached which needs to be improved as quickly as possible. With the remaining surplus, it would be advisable to remove this negative view or weakness now and to become as beneficial as possible for others or for oneself. There is no other way: if one has not stored any good impressions by thoughts, words and actions, and does not do anything meaningful for others, one does not need to hope for a rubber floor that automatically transports oneself back to the top. Having internalized this insight, the deep desire arises to get rid of all dissatisfaction and suffering as quickly as possible, for oneself, one's surroundings and the world.

But it must be done in good style because, without a stiff upper lip, as the British say, and a dignified appearance, one embarrasses people and only a few join in. This pays for one's own life as well. Studies show that self-control is more important for good grades than IQ or talent in athletics.

If one decides to consciously take one's life into one's hands for the improvement of one's karma, one needs the constant insight that it is about the here and now, and that each moment influences the future through the thoughts, words and actions of others and oneself. The responsibility that is associated with this makes it meaningful to discontinue existing bad habits and to strengthen the ripening of good karma. Every moment offers the possibility of letting grow in oneself long-term luck-bringing impressions and views. Harmful behavior in turn loses its attraction when one becomes aware of the karmic impressions one builds up through that.

Whoever does not like to deal endlessly with authorities has surely learned, in today's millimeter societies of laws, rules and regulations, to do as few illegalities with the body as possible. Also, wealth and education oblige because, in this field, disturbing emotions are often seen as a sign of weakness and loss of face. Modern man surely makes the most frequent mistakes through speech, which is, in addition, bound to deep habits.

Along the whole way, it is very useful to avoid the approaching tragedies and to take on several roles in comedies, to the best of one's ability. With more practice, and especially with a frequent use of Buddhist mantras, disturbing emotions slide back and forth as on an oil-film. Finally, without having formed any habits, they fall out of mind, and one can instead call people's attention to nice possibilities. What most people are missing, however, are the methods through which one can remove the seeds of future problems, build up good impressions and dissolve the harmful "I"-misconception, both in this life and beyond. Only with the understanding that, by choosing a high view, one does not simply and unrealistically try to replace something difficult with something beautiful, but that the ultimate truth is unspeakably more beautiful than any dream—only then has one united both the way and goal in oneself.

At long last, the reversal follows when working with harmful actions, words and thoughts, because the mere insight and the simple decision to change the actions and habits are not enough. One should bring the opposite into the world as powerfully as possible. Mind has to be made so rich that the benefit for others automatically emerges and that everyone can find fulfillment in it.

Anyone who, for the good of all beings, tries to reverse all behavior that brings suffering, gets a lot of help on many levels because all parties unconsciously feel that one does not do this just for oneself. Whoever tries to replace self-centered actions with humanitarian ones will—except with bad acquaintances—feel a strong tail wind. The ever-purer view that corresponds to the circumstances, along with the pleasant feedback experiences, provides trust and surplus for further levels of development. To the extent that the habit of referring everything to oneself vanishes, difficulties become tasks, and one remains less and less caught up in expectations and hopes.

Here Buddhists have many tools for powerfully removing the unwanted impressions stored in the mind. The most effective method for this is the meditation on Diamond Mind (Skt. *Vajrasattva,* Tib. *Dorje Sempa*). He is the purifying power of all buddhas and functions like a steam pressure washer, which converts anger and other harmful impressions in mind into beneficial experience and severely weakens ripening karma. In this way, one not only removes the effects but also their causes, and at the same time celebrates the buddha nature of mind.

With increasing practice, one will continuously experience growing clarity and joy, while disturbing emotions and constricting ideas simultaneously lose more and more power and meaning. Finally, the highest view of the Great Seal and further methods of the Diamond Way lift every sound to the level of mantra and make every thought an expression of all-pervading truth.

How Does One Experience Karma?		
One can experience the karma of both happiness and suffering on four different levels:	❶	through pleasant and difficult experiences during death until the new fertilization
	❷	through the endowment of the body: health, intelligence, energy and beauty
	❸	through the surroundings: the country, the culture and the conditions of the family into which one is reborn
	❹	through the tendencies and preferences that one brings along into the new life
How Does One Reduce Negative Karma?		
This happens through four steps in one's attitude:	❶	one realizes the cause of the suffering
	❷	one wishes to remove that which is disturbing
	❸	one takes a firm decision not to do it again
	❹	one consciously decides to do the opposite

SKILLFUL MEANS

Every religion that puts human values and principles above any divine force is very helpful in death, because in its orientation it has to lead to the accumulation of good karma.

How does a Buddhist adjust himself to the beyond-personal levels of mind, which are his goal? With the help of the power-fields of the buddhas and their pure lands. Especially helpful here is the Red Buddha of Limitless Light, who best corresponds to our sensory human world on the levels of liberation and enlightenment. Even if one has little experience with the state of absorption, anyone can call him as a refuge and connect securely with the enlightened power-fields, in order not to be carried away further by the stream of one's impressions in the dying process. Here, one can remember the kindness of one's teachers and the enlightening meaning of their methods and internalize that everything experienced is like the changing images in the mirror or the waves in the ocean. Then mind experiences itself immutably as mirror and ocean, as the timeless experiencer that it always was.

Buddha of Limitless Light and his Pure Land

A pure land is defined as the power-field of a buddha. It is not a place to which one can get physically, but a beyond-personal, unconditioned, joyful-playful state of mind, in which all conditions for liberation and enlightenment are present. Since the illusion of an existing "I" has been dissolved, both ultimate wisdom and great merit will be accumulated fast and powerfully and will not be lost again. Now fullness and richness of mind are experienced, which is the buddha nature of everybody. Every thought is wisdom, simply because it expresses the possibility of space; every sound becomes mantra; and every atom vibrates with joy and is kept together by love.

The best known pure land, accessible to all, is the field of Highest Bliss (Skt. *sukhavati*, Tib. *dewachen*) of the Buddha of Limitless Light.

In prehistoric times this Buddha developed the exceedingly strong wish in connection with his Bodhisattva Promise to create a pure land in which anyone could be reborn only by the power of his wishes. As a result of this attitude, in his enlightenment the Pure Land of Highest Bliss appeared, from which one cannot fall out again. Instead of being driven into a new birth within the circle of the six worlds of experience during the intermediate state, development is guaranteed here. One will return from this realm in a new body for the benefit of others or work as a helpful influence from out of space.

For a rebirth in the power-field of the Buddha of Limitless Light, only four conditions are necessary: the main cause, the deep wish to be born there; the clear calling to mind of the Buddha of Limitless Light and his power-field; avoiding harmful actions; and, finally, as the fourth cause, the enlightened mind (i.e. the wish to attain enlightenment for the benefit of all beings).

For this goal, there are several levels of application that the Buddha gave, according to his students' skills. In addition to the Pure Land school , which is the largest Buddhist school in the world, with over one hundred million followers who repeat the mantra of the Red Buddha as their main practice, one finds, among the most effective methods of the three old "Red Hat" Diamond Way lineages of Tibet, the *Phowa*, which opens the energy channel through the center of the body during life and thus makes the achievement of these levels certain in death.

Because mind is both awareness and energy, countless veils in body, speech and mind lose their hold through the sending up of the consciousness, and liberation comes noticeably closer already in this life. If this certainty arises, one should take into consideration that each rebirth comes with a body and senses that enjoy what is pleasant and do not like what is painful. This creates the illusion of a separation between the experiencer, action and object. Disturbing emotions spread and one makes mistakes.

But if one is wild and doesn't like anything angry, when meeting with Buddha's teaching one experiences joy and natural totality, as if two rivers flow into each other. And if one is basically trusting, the Pure Land is near, and in death, perhaps one will enter something deeply known.

It is impossible to learn to meditate while dying. Therefore, it is a great help to become aware of the dreamlike state of all things during this life, to have understood this at least conceptually, and to have practiced the ability to work with one's mind for years. If the dying person tends to feel sorry for himself, get anxious, angry or excited, one should advise him to align himself compassionately with others, to be thankful, and to remember all the good that binds him with others.

Buddha of Limitless Light

Whoever has meditated during life can trust that both the Phowa practice that one has learned and the Karmapa meditation are a real refuge during the course of dying. They hold and protect one, and their effect is wonderful. One can confidently rest in one's center and let the events go by, in order to apply the appropriate methods in the right moment. For non-Buddhists, it is like an empowerment to witness the certainty of someone dying and his inner peace.

Concerning certain death, one should also decide as early as possible to undermine disturbing emotions and stiff ideas with the existing means during one's lifetime and to recognize the timeless, blissful awareness between and behind the thoughts. At each step toward full realization, one is able to benefit beings so many times better. Since, after death, the untrained mind behaves like a leaf in the wind due to the lack of sensory impressions, one is not able to meditate, and one can only find stability through the already realized absorptions and blessings, one should teach oneself and others that the emerging images are impermanent and do not have any reality.

One should get rid of the attachment to one's life, another major obstacle while dying, as fundamentally as possible. It is the main cause for any fear of death. One should realize as clearly and as early as possible that one cannot take anything with oneself, not the body, partner, friends, possession or the many large and small embosomed things. One should continuously get to know the awareness through view and meditation and be aware as well as possible like always that there exists something that is non-material, timeless, of a nature of highest bliss, and experiences everything external as internal: one's own mind.

Although one can ultimately achieve several bodhisattva levels in each of the intermediate states after death, for Karmapa's students the best way for liberation exists during the dying process. When this is completely used, nothing else is needed.

Whoever meditates daily on the Karmapas' Black Crown and has felt its power-field is able, at the moment when everything turns black, to experience space as his crown. The crossed dorjes then become a gate through which one enters the power-field. Following the symbolism of sun and moon between the stripes with the jewels, the awareness moves upward between the golden clouds, receives the blessing of the vase of long life where the crown merges in its golden stalk, and finally dissolves into the pure land, the red gem on the very top of the crown.

The Black Crown of the Gyalwa Karmapas

CONSCIOUS DYING

The basic questions that one will definitely ask at the end of this book are: Is there a way out of the cycle of life? Can one avoid being reborn countless times? Out of which situation can one be most helpful for other beings?

If one has seldom meditated, one is certainly not in a position to use death in the ways shown by the examples in the following chapter.

However, in Tibetan Buddhism there is Phowa or "Conscious Dying" which one can apply in dying, for oneself as well as for others. One uses the moment of death, when mind separates from the body, either to come from a confused state of mind into a clear, liberated one, or to help others in doing so. As a matter of fact, among the Diamond Way meditations that Buddha passed on to his closest students, this practice is unique in its quickness, applicability, and power. As is generally the case with Buddha's ultimate methods, the benefits from this practice manifest already during one's life, since harmful impressions dissolve for the student, the consciousness solidifies, and the mind becomes clearer. Many

Buddhists therefore say that there is a life before Phowa and a life afterward, and the second part is much better!

Many readers of this book already know this from personal experience, and others hopefully develop the wish, while reading this book, to find as soon as possible a week for this meditation, which is important also for this life.

Although the pure lands, to which one goes after death—and which are experienced more and more strongly during life—still don't signify enlightenment, under all circumstances, one is on the way to liberation, will not fall down from the achieved level of development, and can develop safely according to one's capacities and qualities.

With the word "Phowa" Tibetans imagine a bird, which, trapped under a roof, finds a hatch and swings, freed into space.

Between life and death, depending on ability, one can achieve three enlightened levels of consciousness: Phowa into the Truth State, Phowa into the Joy State, and Phowa into liberating action, the Emanation State.[36]

All meditations in Diamond Way centers are used primarily for mastering life. In addition, by means of their contents, they are also a preparation for death. Phowa is learned specifically for the moment of death, and also applied at the crucial moment for oneself, or for friends, in the way that one has learned.

Milarepa (1040–1123) [37 38]

Milarepa's Words about Death

Those who practice only with their mouth, talk a lot. It looks as if they would know much of the teaching. But, when the time of death comes, their words are thrown into space.

If the Clear Light shines on its own, it is veiled by the blindness of the bad karmas.

The opportunity to experience the Truth State is lost while dying because of one's own confusion.

Even if one spends one's whole life studying the holy scriptures that does not help in the moment when one must take leave.

And those yogis who have not meditated enough wrongly experience appearances of light in mind as sacred radiance.

They cannot bring together the light of mother and son and are always in danger of being reborn in lower realms.

If your body is positioned correctly, the mind remains in the state of absorption, and you feel that there is no more mind, all that remains is contemplation.

Like a starling that flies into the vast empty sky, awareness shines like a pure flower, like a light. Although it is empty, transparent, and radiant, it is just the feeling of a higher state of consciousness.

The one with these good fundamentals sees through to the truth by insight and prays wholeheartedly to the Three Jewels.

He will win the not-I wisdom.

With life roped up by deep definiteness, with the power of kindness and compassion, with the altruistic promise of the Bodhisattva Attitude, he can directly get the clear view, the truth of the Great Enlightened Way.

Nothing can be seen, yet everything is seen.

He sees how false the fears and hopes were; all were in his mind, yet there was nothing.

He arrives at the Pure Land without arrival; he knows the truth state without seeing anything.

Without effort, he naturally knows everything.

Dear son, keep all my statements in mind!

PHOWA INTO THE TRUTH STATE
(Dharmakaya-Phowa)

The moment in which one experiences the nature of mind arises after the coming together of the white light, the red radiant power and the conscious, but non-conceptual states of ignorance. Then, when the Clear Light appears, it is necessary to become one with it and to expand this state into timelessness. If one is able to stay in the state of naked awareness during the melting phase, this will lead to the Truth State, the insight of one's mind as timeless space-awareness. This state is enlightenment itself, and whoever has used the methods of Diamond Way and fearlessly worked with his mind is afterward able to benefit countless beings everywhere.

Every melting phase in daily meditation—where mind has to shine like a diamond and must not stand like a white wall without radiance—strengthens the ability of mind to remain conscious without being conscious of something.

Anyone who has reached a steady experience of the Truth State in life is already beyond death and rebirth. Then one only "seems" to die. Death is like going "from one place to another" or "waking up a little."

With the realization of the highest view—that of the Great Seal—mind's clarity does not break away anymore, and one experiences the primordial purity of conscious space that one has always been and, therefore, could not experience elsewhere. If one can hold this experience of one's own essence, it spreads out and includes past, present, and future, near and far—and one is a Buddha.

PHOWA INTO THE JOY STATE

(Sambhogakaya-Phowa)

If the radiant consciousness of the Truth State cannot be kept, the next opportunity is the Phowa into the Joy State.

When a Westerner wakes up, about sixty-eight hours after the first unconsciousness, the Diamond Way Buddhist experiences, not general confusion, but the buddha realms of the light forms or lamas to whom one was aligned in life. If one is able to recognize a buddha form, one runs to it "like a child to the mother," as the Tibetans say, and melts with it. In this way, one achieves liberation and finds oneself in the power-field of the corresponding buddha. Then one develops, without the constricting ego-illusion, through the bodhisattva levels of joy and richness for the good of all beings.

The dissolving of stiff ideas is only a matter of time now.

In Diamond Way, one already sees the world as a pure land. One does not have to die to go there and, as each mind is Clear Light, one does not have to look for buddhas elsewhere. It is enough, as Buddha said, to polish one's eyes to reach the goal. The main instruction for experiencing the least possible difference between the states of absorption and the times in between, while functioning practically in life, does therefore not only bring happiness but also corresponds to the nature of things.

PHOWA INTO THE EMANATION-STATE

(Nirmanakaya-Phowa)

If one is not able to enjoy the joyful appearances of space and to melt with them, one still has a third opportunity to escape from the cycle of existence. What is special here is that one does not have to have developed very far or meditated particularly much in order to apply this practice successfully in death. In connection with the Phowa, four deeply internalized and constantly lived attitudes bring about a birth in the power-field of Highest Joy. The most important of these is the wish to be born there. Second, it is important to imagine in mind the buddha and his power-field as clearly as possible. The third is that one should avoid harmful actions. The fourth cause is the wish to achieve enlightenment for the benefit of all beings.

If one therefore follows the instructions exactly, has confidence in the teacher and has the determination to help beings in the long term, it will be possible under the special conditions of dying and with the help of blessing to go to liberated levels of consciousness simply by one's attitude and then to develop further until enlightenment. But as one cannot be sure that one can recall this attitude in the process of dying, many want to complete and stabilize these conceptual teachings *(Sutra)* through practice in experience *(Tantra)*.

I know of six different kinds of Phowas for oneself, but there are certainly more. Below, I describe the two that my wife Hannah and I, following the wish of the 16th Karmapa, learned from Ayang Tulku in 1972 in the southern Indian refugee camps. Since 1987, at the request of Tenga Rinpoche and Shamar Rinpoche, I have given courses about twelve times a year for thousands of students around the world. One can do this practice at the moment of death, about sixty-eight hours after death, or during the possible forty-nine days of the bardo.[39]

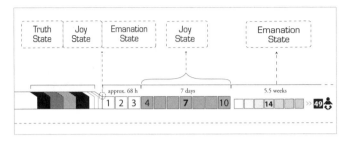

Phowa into the Buddha States

Phowa for Oneself
(Phowa of the Three Consciousnesses)

Phowa is a practice of the Diamond Way. It is open to anyone who is willing to spend five to six days, up to nine hours daily listening to teachings and meditating. However, it requires trust in Buddhist refuge, an empowerment or guided meditation, called *gomlung*, and careful instructions by a trained Diamond Way teacher who is entitled to pass on this practice within his lineage. One meditates on the Buddha of Limitless Light above oneself and develops the wish to enter his power-field, until a visible sign becomes apparent on the top of the skull. It appears as the consequence of the opening of the non-karmic central energy channel in the body and gives one the certainty of being able to go to the pure land, the power-field of this Buddha.

Whoever learns the Phowa should precisely keep in mind the differences between the exercise and the case of emergency —the experience of one's own death—and not forget again. In both cases, as in all Diamond Way practices, he should see the lama as inseparable from the buddha who is called and know that his essence is no different from his light-energy form. Since the teacher is nothing else than the mirror of one's mind and the Phowa allows this cognition, the practitioners need only goal, way, and the "traveling" awareness, in order to go into the pure power-field of this Buddha.

Any kind of Phowa has to be learned well and applied as one-pointedly as possible in the moment of death. It is important at this time not to get carried away by disturbing emotions that emerge, but without distraction to focus on the lama as a representative of the Red Buddha and with undistracted mind to send the consciousness up to him. The body energies released in the course of dying are experienced as very powerful and liberating, as when a giant shoots an arrow from his bow. The connection to the power-field, the Pure Land, lets one hit the target. In that way liberation is most assuredly waiting.

Phowa for Others
(The Hook of Compassion)

With this Phowa one is able to lift deceased friends who were close to the thoughts of Buddhism to a level of development of consciousness from which one cannot fall down again anymore. The deceased then develops further in a closed lotus flower in the Pure Land of the Buddha of Limitless Light.

One learns this meditation only after one has successfully practiced Phowa for oneself. Whoever is looking for methods and blessings for the good of all, should by all means learn these two meditations. Not only does Phowa save beings from fears in the intermediate state, in which mixed impressions appear out of their store-consciousness, but also, in a state of increasing bliss and fulfillment, one circumvents the complete cycle of existence in the conditioned world. The Phowa that bears the name "hook of compassion" brings the greatest benefit within the first half hour after the last breath. During the following sixty-eight hours of unconsciousness, it does not have an effect, but from the third to the tenth day the conditions for it are very good again. If one does not manage to get a feeling of connection to the deceased, one should do Phowa for him once a week, on the day of his death, and repeat mantras such as **OM AMI DEWA HRIH**. The forty-ninth day is the last opportunity to provide direct help for the deceased, and usually heavy cases such as suicides are particularly open for that.

Beyond the intermediate state of death, the scopes of influence are very small. Lopön Tsechu Rinpoche, from whom these teachings of the various Phowas come, could reach the consciousness of a deceased person even after his next rebirth. For such a support, one needs extraordinary insight and realization.

Anyone who has successfully completed a Phowa course can from this moment on help family members, friends, and other loved ones in their deaths, on the way to their secured rebirth at the Red Buddha. It is not advisable for those with Phowa experience to intervene on behalf of strangers whose names, for example, one knows only from obituaries or with whom one has not developed a relationship. Here, one only uses good wishes.

Whoever gives Phowa to the dying should avoid disturbing the attendants in the room as well as possible. In that case one instead goes alone into another room. Even experienced Phowa practitioners have to consider that, under all circumstances, one only starts with the transference of consciousness in one's own

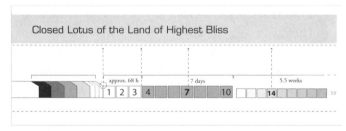

Fortunate moments for Phowa for others

death when one is sure that one is dying. With the hook of compassion one waits, however, until the other person's breathing becomes very disturbed. While doing the Phowa, one imagines being the trusted teacher or buddha. Also, one repeats the practice again and again anew and sends the consciousness to the Buddha of Limitless Light. Nothing comes back again, until the goal is achieved! In this process one wants to avoid shortening the life of the one who is dying by doing Phowa too early; this should not happen at all because a body contains seventy-two thousand buddhas in its power wheels and channels, and is precious.

Since helping others involves strong inner states and very noble actions, the sensitivity of those present is increased. Therefore, moments of suddenly emerging thankfulness, feelings of liberation, and unexpected light experiences are considered as signs of success among the helpers. If the attachment of the deceased is so strong that he does not melt with the Clear Light during the first half hour after the last breathing-out, but falls into unconsciousness while still connected to the body, at the awakening three days after death he will again experience the last impressions that one has given him as a blessing anyway. In this way, he will go through in a better way. Also here each compassionate attempt is worth the effort to give beings access to their inherent freedom.

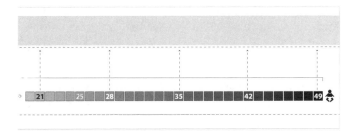

PHOWA COURSES

Although everybody already possesses the ticket to learning Conscious Dying—one was born and thus one will also die someday—besides the intellectual maturity to understand this, certain preparations are necessary for this invaluable practice. For example, in Tibet, Phowa was only given to students who had completed the four Foundational Practices (Tib. *ngöndro*) or promised to do so. The importance of this practice also becomes apparent in the fact that in the traditional three-year retreats it is taught only after two years.

After more than eighty-five thousand Tibetans fled out of their country from Mao's troops in 1959, and many of them died of tuberculosis in the Indian refugee camps, today the access to these teachings is easier. Especially in the humanitarian West, it gets increasingly difficult to find time to meditate between work and distractions. However, since a death follows every life, more than six hundred Diamond Way centers worldwide enable those who want to go to a Buddhist pure land and who agree with the view and goals of the Diamond Way to learn this practice.[40]

New participants prepare best for the Phowa through the so-called Short Refuge and the meditation on the Buddha of Limitless Light (see "Meditations" in the appendix). In the Buddhist centers my competent and experienced students and friends teach and guide these and other Diamond Way meditations.

Those who want to lay the foundation for a relaxed Phowa and make it easier for the lama imagine the Red Buddha of Limitless Light above their heads. He is as transparent as a hologram, has no inner organs, and sits athletically and attractively in the same direction as oneself. One understands him as an expression of unlimited compassion and highest joy and deeply wishes to share his state. At the same time, as one-pointedly as possible, one repeats his mantra **OM AMI DEWA HRIH** one hundred thousand times. In this preparation, many people feel before long that "something" builds up above their heads that wishes them everything good and is where they want to go. If one can additionally do the highly effective purification through the Buddha Diamond Mind and his one hundred- or six-syllable mantra—which removes the roughest obstacles—one has a very good preparation for the Phowa.

At the beginning of the five-day and sometimes—in more difficult circumstances or with thousands of participants —six-day Phowa course, the basic Buddhist knowledge about mind is refreshed. Then the teachings about death, the intermediate state and the refuge are given. After further explanations and questions and a guided meditation, the transmission for the Phowa follows. One meditates three times a day, each time for three hours, spread out over the day, while one sends up the consciousness to the Red Buddha. After nine to twelve such sessions, the "outer" signs are visible on the crown of the new participants' heads, while the "inner" experiences, the doubts and feelings of happiness, diminish and the "secret" sign, the certainty that emerges from this, continues also afterward. The practice brings clear and visible signs. On the skull tiny blood stains, cracks, or pus spots appear, which usually can be seen about eight finger-widths behind the original hairline. When the lama points to the spot or small crack, even a light touch causes a definite pain, which often moves down into the central channel through the body. One does not forget this sensation from then on, and the awareness of the inner axis helps with the posture in all future meditation. Even after the course, a pulling of some hair, or the sense that an ant is running around on the crown, occasionally reminds one of the path that is now open into the pure buddha realms. Here, by the way, the value of the target-oriented Western education becomes obvious: although primarily older Tibetans often have very powerful signs because of their devotion, Westerners often need less time to reach similar results.

As mentioned, the physical appearances are impressive, but for the practitioners it is mainly the inner signs that are noticeable. There are often many strong memories, or impressive mood changes.

Mind can both *know* and *do*. Since awareness and energy come together in mind and make up two sides of the same totality, such a teaching about the power of mind will entail both strong feelings of blessing and happiness, as well as moments in which everything feels like purification or in which the fear of death arises. Deeply stored impressions will be released by repeatedly sending up the mind, and since going out of the body means a giant leap into the unknown—a leap that flows into liberation—the confidence in the teacher and the methods of the Diamond Way also increases.

For many, the short week of their first Phowa course becomes the most significant days of their lives. The joyful faces and the amazed flinching when I touch the opening on their heads give a lasting bond of confidence. Here one gets a deep sense of security concerning one's own dying and an impression of the many wonderful experiences that await one after death. Since these occur especially when one forgets to want or to be something, they are particularly convincing. Beyond concepts, holding or pushing away, images appear in front of the experiencer, are recognized as dream-like and as possibilities of mind, and liberate themselves into space as mere knowledge, without causing expectation or fear. Such experiences of freedom remain stored and develop even more effectively the more one practices. In flashes, the radiant awareness that is between and behind the thoughts and which recognizes them, is experienced. Although the world of habits again snaps shut, it now has more "air" in it, and one can more fluently arise from the narrow *either-or* to the big win-win of the *both-and*.

Having finally arrived at one's center and possessing full strength, one can speak like the Tibetan yogi Rechungpa after a blessing from Milarepa more than eight hundred years ago: "Now I don't need anything from anyone!" The coarsest veils thus fall away, and one has more and more experiences that need no concepts. What is fundamental here is the insight that the experiencer timelessly encompasses birth and death, and a growing trust arises out of this. More than seventy thousand people, to whom I have taught the Phowa worldwide from 1987 to 2010, certainly agree with these descriptions. Nothing is as it was before; everything has meaning and significance.

Often only the teacher sees the third and "secret" characteristic that arises from the Phowa. For the time being it remains hidden to the practitioners, as they are processing enough outer and inner "movies." Also, not everyone is used to exploring the depths of one's own mind. This secret leap into fearlessness does not become visible in the eyes of the people around, as might be expected in our culture. Instead, it shows itself very attractively mostly around the mouth, where dozens of muscles noticeably relax. Often, participants in a course discover only later that they have found surplus in major areas and also have found their personal balance, and that an unshakeable certainty has arisen, allowing them now to watch, with a mild smile, the outer and inner occurrences that would have previously disturbed them or prompted clumsy actions or words.

One should say little about the Phowa practice itself. As with all Diamond Way practices, it draws its power and freshness from the direct transmission of the methods and therefore mere talk harms the result. Since everyone experiences something different, the stories of the the ones who have already finished Phowa fuel false expectations and thus narrow the space for one's own experiences. If someone without previous explanation simply stops by a course, he will see a thousand or more people sitting in an intense state of absorption, or in relaxed bliss, and hear Tibetan chanting. Those who want to learn to die consciously can ask questions and learn the foundation at Buddha's Diamond Way centers.

Although, according to the texts, learning this practice once is enough (if one does not go against one's own teacher), the highest teachers, such as Lopön Tsechu Rinpoche and Shamar Rinpoche, recommend keeping the acquired bond to the Buddha of Limitless Light alive, collecting good impressions and acting humanely, in order to go effortlessly into his power-field at the moment of death.

Different Phowa Practices of Conscious Dying

kind of Phowa		moment	description	requirements
Phowa into the Truth State		ca. 20–30 minutes after the last breathing out	dissolving into the all-pervading awareness of space (*Clear Light*) **Effect:** enlightenment	to be able to rest in the state of naked awareness during the melting-phase
Phowa into the Joy State		3–10 days after death	dissolving into a familiar buddha form **Effect:** liberation	to be able to experience the dream-like state and richness of all phenomena during the building-up and mantra phase
Phowa into the Emanation State	*Phowa of blessing (for oneself)*	During life, during the process of dying and in conscious moments in bardo from the 10th to the 49th day after death	openness and trust in the Buddha of Limitless Light through the Phowa-teacher **Effect:** rebirth in the power field of the Buddha of the Pure Land	wish to be reborn in a liberated state to be able to hold a clear visualization of the Buddhas to avoid harmful actions wish to achieve enlightenment for the benefit of all
	Phowa for others (book of compassion)	In the moment of death or between the 3rd and the 49th day after death	transferring friends and close relatives to the Pure Land of Highest Bliss explanations of the lama *(learned in a course)* **Effect:** rebirth in a closed lotus flower in the Pure Land	meditation on the Buddha of Limitless Light to complete a *Phowa*-course successfully

THE ART OF DYING

The last impressions of a life are very powerful. While the senses are disappearing, one no longer has any influence on the events. They just happen and are experienced differently according to karma. The experiences are then immediate, and this is very confusing for many.

The main experience during the last breathing-out still colors the mind for a while. But if it is not according to the general flow of experience of the dead one, it fades and is mainly replaced by the after-effects of deep wishes and meaningful actions of the last life. Whoever stored a lot of good impressions and removed harmful things will experience fulfillment and meaning, no matter how the last hours of life have been spent. The Southern Buddhist schools attribute great importance to the moment of death, while the Northern ones look more to the sum total of a life. But consciousness itself, recognized by accomplishers—meaning those who experience the mirror behind the pictures—is the ultimate goal.

How does this happen? Both veils, that of the disturbing emotions and that of the stiff ideas, have to tear for it to happen. If the first veil dissolves through recognition of the not-self (i.e. that the "I" is only an illusion), this is called liberation. If the second veil also disappears through insight into the non-existence of a permanent and real outer world, one is enlightened.

The inner experiences of the dying person show more of his essence than the outer circumstances. Tibetans view a painful death as a lightning rod and a useful, final purification, since what is experienced at the end will not ripen later in the intermediate state (if one had a wild youth, for example, grew old happily, but had a painful death). Bodhisattvas and teachers with a lot of compassion are viewed in a similar fashion, but here in relation to their students or other beings: if they die with many diseases or under very difficult circumstances, they purify the future sufferings of their students—through the power of their compassion and the ability to see themselves as inseparable from others.

What exactly is meant by the art of dying? As I see it, it is about three things: One is able to master one's mind in the course of dying in such a way that it remains stable, friendly, and clear. At the same time, one provides an example for others, which encourages them to use the Buddhist methods. Thus one strengthens the trust in others, in their abilities and in the teachings. And to crown it all, in the process of dying, one uses the simplified conditions of mind for one's own liberation or enlightenment.

High Buddhist accomplishers have already recognized the nature of mind during this or previous lives, thus for them dying is nothing extraordinary. Their death is often compared to waking up or to breaking a jar. Since the air inside and outside is the same, there is no difference between awareness here and there. But, for their students and outsiders, meaningful lives with good endings provide proof that a conscious existence pays off. Connected to the teaching that truth is all-pervasive and everyone is ultimately a Buddha, the view of path and goal gives direction in life.

When my noble wife Hannah and I went to the Himalayas in 1968—at that time, tourist-free—and with subsequent annual visits were able to stay there for almost four years, we had the good fortune of being recognized by many of the even then already older meditation masters who had escaped out of Tibet in 1959 as protectors of the teaching, being warmly received and profoundly taught. We later experienced and heard a lot about their passing away, first or second hand. In the context of this book, I would like to give a few examples of some of these teachers, who died consciously in an unusual way. For those who find these ends of life to be too much like a fairy tale, they should know that the stories are not dogmas; whoever dismisses them as "stories" is, therefore, not a bad Buddhist.

In order to stand completely in the teachings, three kinds of confidence are enough: in an absolute goal, the Buddha state; the methods which bring one there; and the realized friends on the way. Whoever wants to develop especially fast, also opens up to a realized teacher and develops devotion to him or her.[41]

Apart from this orientation, the Buddhist does not need anything for his path to enlightenment; everything else, such as the following stories of dying, are additions. One can doubt their reality, understand them metaphorically, or use them as a power source for more meditation.

In the course of the millennia, there were many great masters who consciously showed with their deaths what is possible with Buddha's methods and expressed their deep insight into the emptiness of all phenomena, often as various unusual occurrences in the outer world. When they die, sometimes the sky lights up or rainbows appear. Sometimes they simply dissolve into a rainbow, leaving only hair and nails. In Tibet, such cases of death in which great accomplishers dissolved into rainbow light or remained in meditation posture in their body—often for years after death, without showing signs of decay—were by no means unusual. A contemporary explanation of the rainbow body would be that they transform mass into energy, and quantum physicists like Anton Zeilinger would certainly enjoy seeing their theories realized also at this level.

Sabchu Rinpoche

In the years following the escape of eighty-five thousand
Tibetans from the Chinese over the Himalayas in 1959,
very unusual death reports accumulated. Death came here
primarily through tuberculosis, which afflicted the sensitive
high-altitude lungs of the Tibetan people and carried off
thousands of them in the humid refugee camps south of the
mountains. In the famous Swayambhu Temple of Shamar
Rinpoche, next to the stupa in the Kathmandu Valley, its
director Sabchu Rinpoche, who was also Hannah's and my
teacher, was one of those who died. In 1972 he taught us the
methods of the "peaceful and wrathful breathing" at Karmapa's

special request. Like many accomplishers in the early years, he simply stayed sitting after his death in 1978, without breathing and signs of decay, without being somehow supported from the outside. Meanwhile, his realized energies aggregated around his body as variously colored crystals. He was lucky that no colleague was sent into the room to loudly shout "Pe!" as in the first years after 1959. Through that, even in deep meditation the mind breaks away from the body, so that the body falls over and can then be buried and the room can be used again for other needs. Since the refugees were diligent and in the meantime felt better, they had more space and he could bring his state of absorption to an end undisturbed.

Just before the 16th Karmapa died in fall 1981, he predicted the future parents of Sabchu Rinpoche and stressed that the parents should take the child to the monastery and that it had to be kept very clean. In all the confusion surrounding Karmapa's death, the instructions were unfortunately forgotten. In 1985, when Hannah and I visited Mustang and Bhutan with one of our groups, the intelligent child died of meningitis, caused by tuberculosis. As is usual in such cases, in his following rebirth he chose the same parents again and this time everything was kept most scrupulously clean around him.

The Silversmith Who Becomes
a Rainbow Body

Even lesser-known accomplishers show miracles during dying. A Khampa silversmith from Rumtek, a friend who always gave Hannah and me particularly nice pendants for our malas, had such a damaged back because of Chinese torture that he could not stretch anymore. His legs and body were always at ninety degrees, whether walking or sitting. When he realized that his time had come, he withdrew to a hut and changed the vibrations of everything in his body that contained nerves into energy, by means of the so-called djalu—the rainbow-body meditation. When they went into his locked hut a week later, people found only hair and nails.

The body of the 12th Hambo Lama [42]

The 12th Pandito Hambo Lama Dorzho Itigilow
(1852–1927)

In 2002 I heard the story of a mummified lama in Ulan Ude, Siberia. In 2008, together with many of my students, I was able to see him for the first time. This was made possible through my connection to the present Hambo Lama Ajushejew.

The 12th Pandito Hambo Lama Dorzho Itigilow, who had been born in Czarist Russia in 1852, died in a Buddhist monastery in the steppes of Siberia in 1927. Shortly before his death, he gathered his students around him and asked them to leave the country because of the hard times in the Soviet Union.

In addition, he asked them to check on his body in thirty years. He had his body wrapped with silk cloth and seated himself in the lotus position, in order to die meditating in such a way.

Although Stalin murdered hundreds of Buddhist monks and destroyed forty-six monasteries, after construction of the datsan (monastery) near Ivolginsk, only twenty miles from the capital of Buryatia, Ulan-Ude, the corpse of the deceased Hambo Lama could be dug up thirty years later. His students found him in the lotus position, still completely intact; they could not detect any sign of decay. At that time, however, it was impossible to return him to the monastery, and nobody was allowed to speak about what had happened. So Itigilow's body was lowered into the grave again in a wooden coffin filled with salt.

In early 2002 the deceased was excavated again. His hands were flexible, the eyes closed, his skin leathery but soft. But he was only a little more than a foot tall. Scientific studies revealed a stunning conclusion: The status of the protein components of the tissue was equivalent to that of a living man. The blood had turned into a gel-like substance, traces of embalming were not found, and mummification could also be excluded.[43]

The present Hambo Lama thinks that his predecessor had, through meditation, raised himself to a level of existence that is called shunyata—emptiness. One can assume beyond a doubt that he was able, in the highest degree, to regulate his body and his entire energy system beyond death by meditation, indicating a high realization.

In 2009 we presented the Hambo Lama to the 17th Gyalwa Karmapa and his attendants. All were visibly impressed with this clear example of high realization and, without words, they showed their deepest respect.

Kalu Rinpoche (1904–1989)

"Before we know our life, it is already over and it is time to die. If we do not have a basis for a solid practice available, we helplessly go to our death, in fear and pain."

Kalu Rinpoche

Kalu Rinpoche was a holder not only of the Karma Kagyü transmission, but also of the Shangpa lineage, a school that was founded by Niguma, Naropa's sister or wife (the scholars are not quite sure).[44] In 1973 and 1976, on behalf of the Karmapa, Hannah and I drove him through Europe, where he founded a dozen urban and retreat centers west of the Rhine and blessed ours east of it. A few weeks before his death, in Buddha's place of enlightenment, Bodhgaya in India, he still showed greatness and freshness of mind by critically examining the three-year lama retreats, on which his work had been based for decades. Because of a series of painful results with his students, he demanded that, in the future, they would have to be much more mature and educated before entering.

He spent the last years of his life in the Himalayan foothills in Sonada, near Siliguri on the plains of India, where later a 108-foot-high stupa next to the main road to Assam would be built in his honor. When we took leave of him there during one of his last teachings, he was almost transparent, and apparently was still alive only by his will.

During the last hours in his center, the Indian doctors did not want to give him any peace. But his confidants found a flimsy reason to get them out of the room, closed the door and lifted Kalu Rinpoche into a sitting posture. Unlike some of our other teachers, who kept the mind in the heart, he breathed out deeply once and thus he united with space. In this way, his body remained the original size. After his death his body was dried and covered with gold.[45]

We last saw him sitting in a stupa of the monastery. He was a born teacher. What he said was simple, made sense and was unforgettable, an example like his death.

Born and passed away on the day of Guru Rinpoche

Lopön Tsechu Rinpoche (1918–2003)

The passing away of Lopön Tsechu Rinpoche, who was Hannah's and my first lama, was described to us by his confidante Maggie. She had cared for him for many years, until he left us all on June 10, 2003.

Although Bhutanese, he lived in Nepal and was even invited as a representative of Buddhism to China during the hard years under Mao Tse-Tung. From his first visit to Europe in 1987 until 2003, he supported the buildup of the Diamond Way worldwide.

Lopön Tsechu Rinpoche always remained the benevolent father of our work. With his human depth and his clear-sightedness across cultures, he opened the hearts of count-less people. Among other things, he established nineteen stupas in the West, several of them more than thirty-three feet high, pointing south and aligned to protect Western liberties. Although for years his cardiac output was around forty percent, he traveled around the world with us several times. As he got on the plane in London in 2002, his doctor said, "If you fly now, you will die." "If I do not fly, I will die," Rinpoche answered. "My life is meaningful only when I can help others." When his heart beat with only seventeen percent power and he had to stay with our close friends Caesar and Yoshiko in Bangkok, he still made detailed plans and appointments for the final celebrations of the 108-foot-high Benalmádena stupa on the south coast of Spain that fall. He simply continued to work on as if he would stay with us. He never mentioned his approaching death and died quietly and simply, but mastering the situation, just as he had shown his entire life. He looked Maggie in the eyes and stopped breathing. There was peace in the room, but his activity remained unbroken, and his power-field is still with us today.

Hannah Nydahl (1946-2007)

My wife, Hannah, cherished since 1968 as the "mother," protectress, and confidante for dozens of Tibetan lamas in the West as well as the East, was even more impressive in death than can be vaguely perceived in my books. Instead of limiting herself to the thought that her prosperous life would be cut off too early, she enjoyed her remaining time and kept on using it for the good of others. She had no fear and also trusted in this situation, that everything makes sense and would happen in the right way. She publicly said goodbye at the New Year's celebration in Stuttgart in 2007, thanked all the students and gave them great confidence for their further way.

Humble as she was, she only asked for two things: to spend the rest of the time together with me, and to do this in Copenhagen, our home. It happened, as always in her life; all conditions came together as if on their own.

Her female students touchingly looked after her needs and did not leave her side. Three Buddhist doctors gave her the necessary medical care without hesitation, so she could spend the entire time in the Copenhagen center. Also, everyone there adjusted completely to her and offered her the setting to manage what was still possible for her.

The 17th Karmapa Thaye Dorje had already said goodbye to her before Christmas. He made a special trip to Kempten by car, all the way from southern Spain, and we spent the whole day with him. Shamar Rinpoche, the second highest lama in the Karma Kagyü lineage, visited her in Copenhagen on the tenth of March. On this day everyone realized that Hannah would die. Only the urgent advice of our doctors, who lived in the room next door and took care of her day and night in the best possible way, kept the friends, coming from all over the world, from laying siege to the stairs to her room.

Extremely modest as usual, she spoke about her approaching death only once during all these months: a day before she stopped talking, together with me she passed on her work in KIBI (the Karmapa Buddhist Institute in Delhi) to Kerstin and many other things to Caty. Hannah happily signed the purchase agreement for our Europe Center and then withdrew from the friends for this life.

Along with the time of hope of recovery before the New Year, the disease gave Hannah and me five months of deep exchange and we were conscious of the fact that in future lives we would work together as a couple for the Diamond Way.

Hannah died sitting in my arms on the night of April 1, 2007. She was clinically dead fifteen times—over a minute without heartbeat or breath—as the two Buddhist doctors in the room confirmed. Every time she came back through her willpower. At the sixteenth time, when it became clear that she should go now, I made Phowa and asked her to move on. The smile on her face the next morning said it all. It was as if she had just tasted something wonderful.

Being the wisdom behind our common work, she has influenced countless people with her gentle love. For me she is present always and everywhere as the radiant state of inspiration. May many become like her.

The 16th Gyalwa Karmapa (1924–1981)

"Nothing happens," was the 16th Karmapa Rangjung Rigpe Dorje's answer to the question of what happens during dying.

At the summer solstice in 1980 in Colorado, USA, while saying goodbye to us, Karmapa said: "Come again on the first day of the eleventh month of the next year." And he confirmed that the time corresponded to the Western and not to the Tibetan calendar. We were astonished, but understood later why he kept us away from him for a while. We were, of course, his main students among the fresh new Buddhists in the West and, above all, as a teacher in charge I was only qualified to represent him as hero of the moment, as powerful and radiant as we knew him up to then. "You can bring your friends along," he added. So that was how it happened that Hannah and I traveled with more than a hundred friends into the Himalayas, while the following events were happening in the American hospital near Chicago.[46] It is not surprising that, as the "King of the Yogis of Tibet," Karmapa deeply impressed both his students and representatives of Western science with his death. Even in life the 16th Karmapa Rangjung Rigpe Dorje, as well as his earlier incarnations, embodied the activity of all Buddhas.

Born in 1924 in Eastern Tibet, he saved the transmissions and the most important relics of his lineage from the attacking Chinese with an impressive escape from Tibet in 1959. As a basis for the continuation of the Old-School teachings of Tibet, he first built up the big center of Rumtek in Sikkim in 1961–65. Then, several times from 1973 until his death in 1981, with his Western students he visited North America and Europe, where his great openness for lay Buddhism solidified. The rest of the time he spent mainly in Sikkim and, through frequent teachings, crown ceremonies and empowerments, he saved the transmissions of the Kagyü School. Certainly to bless the West once again, where he predicted major developments for his teachings, and to show the world the effect of the Diamond Way, in mid-October 1981, already very ill, he accepted an invitation to Hong Kong and afterward to the United States. He died on November 5, near Chicago from half a dozen deadly diseases. He had invited Hannah and me to Rumtek precisely for the first of November, and his body arrived there in a helicopter a few days later. On December 20, 1981 the body was burned with the miracles that are described in *Riding the Tiger.*

He donated the last eighteen days of his life in the hospital to science, allowing the doctors to treat him with their strongest medications. At the beginning, Dr. Levy—not a Buddhist—was still amazed that his patient never complained of pain and, despite his serious illness, was always concerned about the happiness of others. He always radiated a powerful and deep love, concerned himself for the well-being of doctors and nurses, and made jokes. The longer they looked after him, the more impressed they were by him, and the closer death approached, the more they all had to question their entire medical world view. For the participants, it was a constant teaching for what a focused and powerful mind makes possible. Dr. Levy, for example, had the feeling that Karmapa deliberately delayed his death so that all could get acquainted with it and observe the process and learn from it.

Karmapa apparently experienced his body as a tool and wanted to teach his students and the world something important. Thus he kept his concern for others until the last moment. Especially for the doctors and nursing staff, this was often unusual because, instead of meeting a poor, weak, needy patient, Karmapa's attention was always lovingly directed to all the others. His radiance and warmth remained completely unchanged and overwhelmed all the visitors and the hospital staff, even when his body was getting weaker and he was finally dying. Normally, the staff of an intensive care unit avoids a close personal relationship with the patient, in order to be able to work more professionally. But, with Karmapa, everything was different: everyone was deeply touched. His state of mind had an incredible strength and unshakability, which radiated on everybody and which no one could explain. His presence left nobody untouched. One could simply not understand that, regardless of his pain, Karmapa behaved very differently from how dying people usually do.

After a few days, Karmapa's condition deteriorated dramatically. He had difficulties with breathing, was coughing blood, and his blood pressure dropped rapidly. From a medical perspective he showed all the symptoms of an immediate death. For this reason Dr. Levy asked the present lineage holders to make their last visit to Karmapa. However, forty-five minutes later they came back out of his room, completely relaxed and said that Karmapa had laughed at their "farewell visit" and cheerfully explained to them that he did not yet intend to die. When Dr. Levy went into the room, Karmapa was sitting upright in his bed with eyes wide open and asked how he was doing. Within half an hour he had stopped bleeding and all his vital signs were stable again and at normal levels. Karmapa's willpower was obviously so strong that he could determine when he would leave the body. And so far he was not ready.

Ten days later his blood pressure fell steeply again and could also not be stabilized with medication. While all the signs again suggested death within a few minutes and the doctors fought for his life, Karmapa gave a friendly smile, only to chat with the doctors two hours later, again with normal blood pressure and sitting upright in bed.

No one in the hospital had experienced such a thing before: a patient with terminal cancer and massive lung inflammation actually does not recover, not to mention that he, recovered, sits upright in bed, and is happy and friendly.

When the Karmapa died the following day, he surprised the doctors one last time. When his heart stopped early in the morning, they immediately started with the resuscitation and were able to stabilize Karmapa for half an hour. Finally, however, the blood pressure entirely plummeted and it came to the final cardiac arrest. The doctors resuscitated Karmapa for forty-five minutes again, but on the heart monitor one could clearly see how the heart failed more and more and also no longer responded to direct injections. Finally, the doctors gave up, recorded Karmapa's death, and left the room. Already clinically dead, Karmapa then simply switched on the machines that were connected to him.

When the nursing staff wanted to pull out the feeding tube a quarter hour later, they saw on the heart monitor that Karmapa's blood pressure again was at 140 to 80 and his pulse was regular. As Dr. Levy arrived, he had the feeling that he would faint—the event was so far outside his usual realm of experience. One of the older Rinpoches patted him reassuringly on the shoulder and said, "It is impossible, but it happens."

One had the impression that, one hour after his heart had finally stopped beating by itself and fifteen minutes after the doctors had given up on him, Karmapa came back again to see if this body could still carry his mind or not. But that was still not enough: even after his death, Karmapa did not stop amazing Western physicians. Forty-eight hours after his death his heart region was still warm and his skin remained smooth. Since the hospital, as an exception, granted permission to leave Karmapa's body undisturbed in the hospital room, he remained in this deep state of absorption for two more days, until he was flown to Sikkim. During a stopover in London, the zinc coffin was adorned with flowers by students.

The "King of the Yogis," the 16th Karmapa, Rangjung Rigpe Dorje, "Diamond of the Self-arisen Ultimate Truth," had also drawn miracles from his sleeve in previous incarnations in connection with his death. Following this tradition, Karmapa, who had completely shaken the doctors in the US by his games with the laws of nature, four days already clinically dead and flown halfway around the world in a coffin, merrily continued his miracles. He had the ability, without any disintegration in the warm weather and with the many butter lamps, to shrink his body to the size of less than two feet within forty days, until December 20, 1981. His head made up a third of his size and, when I looked at him before the burning and said goodbye, he was deeply gray, but intact and easily recognizable.

The kind of meditation that Karmapa used points to the realization of his mind. In this state, one can choose one of three meditations to melt with the Truth State. With the *tudam* (*tu* means heart, *dam* bond, i.e. that mind remains bound in the heart) used by Karmapa, one can even recognize as an outsider that something very unusual happens here to the body, which of course gives much confidence in the power of mind.[47] In this meditation one anchors one's mind in the Truth State in the course of dying and experiences naked awareness itself. Here, the experiencer dwells in the heart and, at the same time, becomes completely clear and boundless. Then space-awareness inside and outside is no longer separated, and huge power and unending timeless vastness can be experienced. Here present, past and future melt effortlessly into timeless insight. From this level, one is able to be reborn for the good of beings in any place, take countless bodies, and help wherever beings have a connection with one.

When his body was burned on the main building of Rumtek and with a clear view over the Gangtok Valley and the Eastern Himalayas, there were two circular rainbows around the sun. Karmapa's heart rolled out of the oven down to Lopön Tsechu Rinpoche, who was standing there opposite us around the burning stupa.

The life and death of the 16th Karmapa was the ultimate proof of the richness and possibilities of mind inherent in everybody. His example is still the motor for my students and me in the West. The wishes that we made during this burning still fulfill themselves today. During his absence, the Diamond Way grew and matured across the world. Today, the 17th spiritual reincarnation Gyalwa Karmapa, Trinley Thaye Dorje, continues this transmission in good style.

The 17th Gyalwa Karmapa Trinley Thaye Dorje

Meditations

....

Everybody knows meditation. The moments in life when one receives a gift, when joy comes out of one's own power and everything is simply meaningful, are meditation experiences. Without noticing, the ocean of mind comes to rest and one sees clearly; the dust falls from the inner mirror and one understands.

What brings so much fulfillment, without adding anything, is one's own mind—the awareness of this very moment. This state can consciously be made to last.

In order that the information one has read can fall from the head into the heart, here are five meditations that can be done without the guidance of a teacher. Those who like to meditate with others can learn this in the more than 600 Karma Kagyü Diamond Way centers around the world.

Basically, one sits up straight in every meditation, either on a chair or cross-legged on the floor, in a pleasant, quiet room. One keeps the back straight, but not stiff. The hands rest in the lap or on the knees. Then one follows the text. If thoughts appear now and then which have nothing to do with the meditation, one doesn't take further note of them. They will dissolve just as they have appeared.

The following meditations actually correspond to different levels of development in the Buddhist teachings, but they can be used by anyone. Although simple to practice, they contain everything important from all of Buddha's paths.

The meditations generally strengthen pleasant characteristics of the practitioner. Both in the meditation on Loving Eyes and on the Karmapa, the great variety of the Diamond Way becomes apparent: either one consciously aims for enlightened qualities such as love and compassion in the meditation on Loving Eyes or one concentrates on a Buddha in the form of the 16th Karmapa in order to act more and more powerfully for the best of all. One can also imagine a golden buddha form instead of the Karmapa. Finally, one can prepare for the courses of Conscious Dying (Phowa), mentioned in the book, by using the meditation on the Buddha of Limitless Light, which is also a Diamond Way meditation.

In the beginning it is better to do a guided meditation in a group in order to get to know the practice correctly and to clarify issues. If one wants to follow the Buddhist path, it is necessary to receive oral explanations and transmissions about the meditations from a teacher. In every Diamond Way Center, there are public meditations and introductory evenings.

Practice effortlessly and enjoy!

Meditation on Light and Breath

In this meditation one practices pacifying the mind and creating a distance from the everyday, constantly tumbling down worlds of experience. That way one gradually gets out of the agitated state of mind that can easily lead to suffering-bringing thoughts, words and actions. This "holding and pacifying" kind of absorption is compared with tethering a horse: It now stays at one point, instead of chasing everyone and learns to see what is. If one has often enough noticed the impermanent games of the world, they no longer influence one and one has gained the first level of peace of mind. It is not only useful for this purpose, but it works very well as a basis for all further meditations.

We sit comfortably, either on a cushion or a chair. Our hands rest in our lap, the right on the top of the left, palms up and thumbs touching lightly. We keep our back straight without tightness and our chin pulled in a little.

First, we calm our mind. We feel the formless stream of air coming and going at the tips of our noses, letting thoughts and sounds go by without holding on to them.

Now, we will meditate in order to experience mind and to gain distance from our disturbing emotions. Only then, can we really be useful for others.

A foot and a half in front of our nose, there now appears a clear, transparent light. While we breathe in, the light moves in a stream down through the center of our body. On its way, the clear light turns ever more red. Stopping briefly, four fingers below the navel, the transparent light has become totally red. Then we exhale naturally, the red light moves upward and becomes gradually more blue. A foot and a half in front of us, the transparent, blue light becomes clear, and we inhale it once more.

We hold this awareness without tension, while our breath comes and goes naturally.

If it's difficult to see the colors, we simply think: clear light when we inhale, red light when the light stops below the navel and blue light when we exhale.

After a while, we may also focus on the vibrations of our breath.

While inhaling, we hear the syllable **OM**.

While holding the light below the navel, we hear a deep **AH**.

While exhaling, we hear the vibration of **HUNG**.

We stay with this for as long as we like.

Pause

At the end of the meditation, the world appears fresh and new. We wish that all the good that just happened may become limitless, radiate out to all beings everywhere, remove their suffering and give them the only lasting joy, the realization of the nature of mind.

The Meditation of Giving and Taking

In this meditation one sows good impressions into the mind so that one is able to naturally help others. One adjusts to the difficulties and suffering of beings and transforms them into love for the good of all beings. Since one knows about egolessness, suffering cannot harm one. The development of compassion for others is the goal of this basic meditation of the Great Way.

We feel the formless stream of air that comes and goes at the tips of our noses and let thoughts, feelings, and sounds pass by without evaluating them.

When mind becomes calm, we take refuge in the Buddha as our goal, his Teachings as our way, and in the Bodhisattvas, our friends and companions on the way. We now want to meditate so we become able to benefit all beings and understand the non-reality of all conditioned existence.

We experience the pain of all beings as a black cloud that surrounds them and we fearlessly inhale it. Once the cloud reaches our heart, our compassion and understanding of emptiness transforms it into shining clear light. This streams back to all beings as we exhale. It shines over them and brings them every happiness. We do this as long as it feels comfortable.

When we finish the meditation, we wish that all the good just created may benefit all beings.

The goal of this meditation is to plant good impressions in one's mind in order to benefit others.

Loving Eyes Meditation

Loving Eyes

Loving Eyes (Tib. *Chenrezig*, Skt. *Avalokiteshvara*) represents the compassion of all buddhas. One of his most frequent appearances is as a white, four-armed form. Meditating on him is about completely realizing his compassion and love by becoming one with him.

The four arms indicate that this is not a solid, worldly appearance. They symbolically represent the four kinds of love: love, compassion, sympathetic joy and equanimity.

His attributes (crystal mala, cloths, lotus flower and many more) and their meaning have an effect on the subconscious without words.

The focus is his mantra **OM MANI PEME HUNG**. In Nepal and Tibet it is certainly the most often recited and one sees it everywhere and always carved in stone. While turning the prayer wheels clockwise, often near a stupa—the small form of them in the hand, or using a mala—one wishes everything good for all beings. The mantra has the same meaning in this meditation.

We feel the formless stream of air at the tips of our noses and let thoughts and feelings pass without evaluation.

The Four Thoughts

Then we focus on the four basic thoughts, which turn mind towards liberation and enlightenment.

We recognize our precious opportunity in this life, that we can benefit countless beings through the methods of a Buddha. Few people ever meet Diamond Way teachings and even fewer are able to use them.

We remember the impermanence of everything composite. Only the unlimited, clear space of mind is lasting, and it is uncertain how long conditions will remain for recognizing it.

We understand causality. That it is up to us what will happen. Former thoughts, words and actions became our present state, and right now we are sowing the seeds for our future.

Finally, we see the reasons for working with mind. Enlightenment is timeless highest bliss, and we cannot benefit others while confused or disturbed ourselves.

Therefore, we now open up to those who can teach us.

Refuge

To bring all beings to enlightenment, we take refuge:
In the Buddha, mind's full development;
In his Teachings, which bring us there;
In the Bodhisattvas, our friends on the way;
And especially in the Lama. He unites blessing, methods
and protection and is needed for our fast development.
Here he appears in his compassionate form as Loving Eyes.

Building-up Phase

Above our head and the heads of all beings, mind's
natural purity expresses itself as a fully open lotus flower. It is
transparent and slightly rainbow colored. Within each
lotus, the basic intelligence of beings manifests as a radiant
disc of the moon lying flat. At the center of each moon-disc,
enlightened love now condenses as a white Tibetan letter
HRIH (or H-R-I-H written from the top and down).

From this syllable, transparent, rainbow light shines out
to the countless buddhas throughout space. The light also
touches unenlightened beings everywhere and dissolves all
their suffering.

Now, the rainbow light is charged with the blessing of

the buddhas and the happiness of all beings. It returns to the **HRIH** syllables above our heads. In an instant, they become forms of four-armed Loving Eyes. He sits in full meditation posture and is radiant like moonstone. These light-forms sit above all beings.

A radiant moon-disc supports Loving Eyes' back. He wears the ornaments of a bodhisattva. His outer right hand is at shoulder level. It holds a crystal mala that lifts all beings out of the conditioned world. His two middle hands hold the jewel of enlightenment to his heart. His outer left hand holds a lotus flower that opens at his left ear. It shows his absolute purity. Loving Eyes smiles kindly on all beings. A deerskin is draped over his left shoulder signifying that he possesses the kindness of this animal and will never harm anyone. The five-colored cloth around his hips represents all levels of initiation. His meditation posture signifies that he works between confusion and liberation to benefit beings.

Above the head of each form of Loving Eyes, sits the red Buddha of Limitless Light (Tib. *Öpame*, Skt. *Amitabha*). Both look with compassion on all beings expressing the non-discriminating love of all buddhas.

During the classical invocation to awaken the power of Loving Eyes, we say: "You noble one with the faultless white body, the perfect Buddha is seated above your head. With eyes of compassion, you see all beings; Loving Eyes we take refuge in you."

Now, Loving Eyes empowers us. From his forehead, a clear light shines out in an arc into our forehead and gives us the

Vase Initiation. From his throat, a red light comes in an arc into our throat and gives us the Secret Initiation. From his heart, a blue light then falls in an arc into our heart and gives us the Wisdom-Awareness Initiation. Finally, all three lights enter us at the same time, and we receive the Ultimate Initiation of the Great Seal.

After this transmission, the light-forms of Loving Eyes above melt down into all beings and ourselves. In an instant, we become Loving Eyes. The world is his pure land, radiant with meaning. Every sound is the vibration of his mantra, and every thought is highest wisdom, simply because they can occur. At heart-level, in the middle of our transparent light-form, rests an open lotus flower with six petals. Each holds one of the six syllables of his mantra arranged clockwise with **OM** towards the front. Upon the center of the flower, lies a flat disc of the moon. In the middle of the moon-disc, stands the Tibetan letter **HRIH**.

While all beings and ourselves repeat the mantra **OM MANI PEME HUNG** for as long as we wish, vivid, rainbow light shines from the mantra into the hearts of all beings and fills space completely.

OM MANI PEME HUNG

(Repeat the mantra for as long as you wish)

Completion Phase

When we stop saying the mantra, all the pure lands are absorbed into the forms of Loving Eyes. These then dissolve into light and radiate from all directions into our own four-armed transparent form, which disappears into the seed syllable **HRIH** at heart-level. Then, the petals of the lotus flower and their mantra syllables return to space in a clockwise direction. Next, the center of the flower and the moon disc dissolve. Finally, the **HRIH** letter disappears from the bottom upwards until only one tiny point is left. Nothing else remains of the conditioned world. In a flash, this point of light vanishes and there is now only awareness without center or limit. We stay as consciously as possible in this basic state.

Pause

Then, like a fish jumping from water, again a pure world appears. All beings and ourselves have buddha nature. All sounds are the mantra of Loving Eyes and all thoughts highest wisdom.

Dedication
We decide to keep this understanding in all life's situations and wish that the good impressions that just appeared become limitless. May they bring all beings the only lasting joy, that of knowing mind.

Meditation on the 16th Karmapa

The 16th Gyalwa Karmapa

Hannah and I were given this meditation by the 16th Karmapa himself. He asked us several times to spread this practice in the Western world because it is easy to understand for the students there, highly effective, briefly worded and suitable for everyday life. This meditation on the teacher, which constitutes the basic method of the Diamond Way, has the highest level of realization as a result. Anyone who daily adjusts to enlightened qualities with a wish to also be able to benefit others here has a valuable tool.

We feel the formless stream of air at the tips of our noses and let thoughts and feelings pass without evaluation.

The Four Thoughts

Then we focus on the four basic thoughts, which turn mind towards liberation and enlightenment.

We recognize our precious opportunity in this life, that we can benefit countless beings through the methods of a Buddha. Few people ever meet Diamond Way teachings and even fewer are able to use them.

We remember the impermanence of everything composite. Only the unlimited, clear space of mind is lasting, and it is uncertain how long conditions will remain for recognizing it.

We understand causality, that it is up to us what will happen. Former thoughts, words and actions became our present state, and right now we are sowing the seeds for our future.

Finally, we see the reasons for working with mind. Enlightenment is timeless highest bliss, and we cannot benefit others while confused or disturbed ourselves.

Refuge

To bring all beings to enlightenment, we take refuge:
In the Buddha, mind's full development;
In his Teachings, which bring us there;
In the Bodhisattvas, our friends on the way;
And especially in the Lama, here the 16th Karmapa.
He unites blessing, methods and protection, and is needed for our fast development.

Building-up Phase

Now, out of space in front of us, condenses the golden, transparent form of the 16th Karmapa, a radiant field of energy and light.

Karmapa wears the Black Crown, the shape of which can awaken mind's deepest awareness. His face is golden and mild. He sees us, knows us and wishes us everything good.

His hands hold a dorje and a bell crossed at his heart. They express the state of compassion and wisdom inseparable. Seated in meditation posture, he is surrounded by light.

Karmapa unites space and bliss and is the activity of all buddhas. His essence is here whether a clear image is perceived or not. We strongly wish to accomplish his enlightened qualities for the benefit of all.

Karmapa knows our wish. He smiles and comes ever closer through space. He now remains at a pleasant distance in front of us.

"Dearest Lama, essence of all buddhas, please show us the power which removes the ignorance and obscurations of all beings and ourselves. Let mind's timeless light be recognized inside us."

A strong, clear light radiates from between Karmapa's eyebrows and enters the same place in our forehead. Our head is filled with powerful, clear light.

The light dissolves all disturbing impressions in brain, nerves and senses. All causes and imprints of harmful actions disappear, and our body relaxes. It becomes a conscious tool for protecting and helping others. We retain the clear light for as long as we wish and experience the syllable **OM**.

(Hold light and vibration)

Emanating from Karmapa's throat, a radiant beam of red

light streams out. It enters our mouth and throat.

The light dissolves all difficulties in our speech. All impressions of harmful and confused words disappear, and we become conscious of our speech. It is now compassion and wisdom, a powerful tool for benefiting others. Along with the red light, we experience the syllable **AH.**

(Hold light and vibration)

From the heart level in the center of Karmapa's transparent body, an intense, blue light shines out. It fills the middle of our chest.

Everything harmful now leaves our mind. Disturbing feelings and stiff ideas dissolve, and our mind becomes spontaneous joy. It is space and bliss inseparable. Together with the blue light, we experience the syllable **HUNG.**

(Hold light and vibration)

Now, all three lights enter us at the same time. Clear light fills our head, red light our throat and blue light our heart center. We rest effortlessly in the oneness of all phenomena.

(Hold the three lights together)

We may now use the mantra **KARMAPA CHENNO.** It means power of all Buddhas work through us.

KARMAPA CHENNO

Completion Phase
In front, Karmapa's golden form and his Black Crown dissolve into rainbow light.
It falls on us, is everywhere and all form disappears.

There is now only awareness with no center or limit.

(Rest in the nature of mind)

Whatever may appear is the free play of space.

(Rest in the nature of mind)

Activity Phase

Now, our surroundings, this world and all worlds appear, perfect and pure. Everything vibrates with joy and is kept together by love. All is fresh and meaningful, radiant with unlimited potential.

Beings manifest near and far. They are female or male buddhas, whether they know it or not.

Sounds are mantras and all thoughts wisdom, for the sole reason that they can happen.

We feel our own body condense out of space. It is power and joy. Something essential has happened. Before, we were our body and thus vulnerable to old age, sickness, death and loss. Now we *have* our body. Body and speech are conscious tools for benefiting others.

Our true essence, and we know that now, is the time-less awareness beyond center and limit, which playfully manifests all.

Dedication

We decide to keep this understanding in all life's situations and wish that the good impressions that just appeared become limitless. May they bring all beings the only lasting joy, that of knowing mind.

Meditation on the Buddha of Limitless Light
(preparatory meditation for participation in a Phowa course)

Nothing is more important than mastering our death. Through the power of the Red Buddha of Limitless Light, one can shift into the realm of Highest Joy during the process of dying. Here is an access to this unsurpassable gift. Whoever wants to join the meditation course on Conscious Dying should be familiar with the following meditation and its images. Once one strives for permanent results, habitualness deepens the experience. Therefore, I am always very happy when participants have repeated the short mantra given here 100,000 times before their first Phowa.

We feel the formless stream of air at the tips of our noses and let thoughts and feelings pass without evaluation.

The Four Thoughts
Then we focus on the four basic thoughts, which turn mind towards liberation and enlightenment:

We recognize our precious opportunity in this life, that we can benefit countless beings through the methods of a Buddha.

Few people ever meet Diamond Way teachings and even fewer are able to use them.

We remember the impermanence of everything composite. Only the unlimited clear space of mind islasting and it is uncertain how long conditions will remain for recognizing it.

We understand causality. That it is up to us what will happen. Former thoughts, words and actions became our present state and right now we are sowing the seeds for our future.

Finally, we see the reasons for working with mind. Enlightenment is timeless highest bliss, and we cannot benefit others while confused or disturbed ourselves. Therefore we now open up to those who can teach us.

Refuge

To bring all beings to enlightenment, we take refuge:
In the Buddha, mind's full development,
In his Teachings which bring us there,
In the Bodhisattvas, our friends on the way,
And especially in the Lama, here the 16th Karmapa. He unites blessing, methods and protection and is needed for our fast development.

Building-up Phase

Above our head and at a reachable distance there now arises a fully open lotus flower. A flat disc of the moon is lying inside it. Upon it the Buddha of Limitless Light sits facing in the same direction as we are. He is athletic and luminous and shines like a mountain of rubies in the light of a thousand suns.Radiant and beautiful beyond all concepts, his state is the fulfilment of any possible wish.

Being in essence the Karmapa and our root lama, he is seated in the position of meditation. His hands hold a bowl of lapis lazuli in his lap with the nectar of highest bliss.

To his right, above our right shoulder and smaller than the Buddha of Limitless Light, stands the united compassion of all Buddhas, the white four-armed form of Loving Eyes (Tib. *Chenrezig*, Skt. *Avalokitesvara*). To his left and above our left shoulder stands Diamond in Hand (Tib. *Channa Dorje*, Skt. *Vajrapani*), the united power of all Buddhas, in his peaceful light blue form. He holds a bell to his heart and a dorje towards Limitless Light. The three central forms are surrounded by the lamas of all Phowa lineages.

Repeating the mantra for as long as possible, we hold our awareness with the pure land above, and strongly wish to enter the heart of the Red Buddha.

OM AMI DEWA HRI

Completion Phase

When we finish the repetitions, the lamas and the pure land above melt into the white and the blue bodhisattvas.

These dissolve into the Buddha of Limitless Light and become one with him. Then he becomes light and streams down into us. Like water flowing into water, there is no separation. The world is a pure land. Beings appear everywhere. All having the buddha nature. We are our habitual form, now without weakness or disease.

We decide to keep this understanding in all life's situations and wish that the good impressions that just appeared become limitless. May they bring all beings the only lasting joy, that of knowing mind.

Endnotes

1. Norman Doidge, *The Brain That Changes Itself: Stories of Personal Triumph from the Frontiers of Brain Science* (New York: Penguin Books, 2007).

2. The "body-soul problem" is a European concept. According to the philosophical traditions in Asia, the separation into mind and body is illusionary and without meaning.

3. Cardiologist Pim van Lommel interviewed 344 patients at ten Dutch medical centers who had been clinically dead after a cardiac arrest and were able to be resuscitated successfully. Van Lommel concludes that (a) clear consciousness is possible even in periods of cardiac arrest and the complete cessation of cerebral blood flow and (b) consciousness cannot be seen as a result of brain activity. See P. van Lommel, *Consciousness Beyond Life: The Science of the Near-Death Experience* (New York: HarperCollins, 2010).

4. Probably the simplest example of the non-dual "both-and" quantum logic is the wave-particle duality. According to this concept, light can be seen as a wave or as a particle, depending on the perspective. The most exciting characteristic of the quantum field theory becomes apparent in the Casimir-effect:

Even if an area of space seems to be completely empty, it bubbles with virtual particles that emerge out of space, exist for a short period of time and disappear back into space.

5. Z. Rosenkranz and B. Wolff, *Albert Einstein: The Persistent Illusion of Transience* (Jerusalem: Magnes Press, 2007).

6. R. Sheldrake, *Journal of the Society for Psychical Research*, 68(1), 2001, 168–172.

7. "I believe we have to abandon the idea that mass and energy are primary. It may indeed be that the foremost is just information." See A. Zeilinger, *Einsteins Schleier: Die neue Welt der Quantenphysik*, (Munich: Verlagsgruppe Random House, 2003) and A. Zeilinger, *Einsteins Spuk: Teleportation und weitere Mysterien der Quantenphysik* (Munich: C. Bertelsmann Verlag, 2005).

8. The Nobel Prize for Physics in 2007 for Giant Magnetoresistance (GMR) was awarded to Albert Fert (born in 1938 in France) and Peter Grünberg (born in 1939 in Germany). Fert and Grünberg almost simultaneously discovered the GMR, independently from each other in 1987–88.

9. Anton Zeilinger, in a personal talk with me on April 3, 2006: "It seems that information is something which is beyond the scope of time and space."

10. Tsele Natsok Rangdröl (Erik Pema Kunsang, trans.), *The Mirror of Mindfulness*, Updated Edition: *The Cycle of the*

Four Bardos (Rangjung Yeshe Publications, 2010).
Tenga Rinpoche, *Übergang und Befreiung,* (Khampa Buchverlag, 1996).

11. Ole Nydahl, *The Way Things Are: A Living Approach to Buddhism for Today's World* (Washington: Mantra Books, 2008).

12. Gampopa (Khenpo Könchog Gyaltsen Rinpoche, trans.), *The Jewel Ornament of Liberation: The Wish-fulfilling Gem of the Noble Teachings* (New York: Snow Lion Publications, 1998).

13. See "Meditations."

14. See Ole Nydahl, *Ngöndro: The Four Foundational Practices of Tibetan Buddhism* (Grass Valley, CA: Blue Dolphin Press, 1990).

15. A series of four different meditations that prepares mind for more profound meditations. See Ole Nydahl, 1990.

16. *Manibhadra* is one of the 84 mahasiddhas. These great accomplishers of old India, both men and women from diverse social classes, combined their Buddhist practices with their everyday lives in a unique way and are, therefore, important examples for all laypeople and accomplishers.

17. See S. Lyubomirsky, *The How of Happiness: A New Approach to Getting the Life You Want* (New York: Penguin Press, 2008).

18. Graphics by Malte von Tiesenhausen.

19. "Dead, but a brain wave lingers on," *New Scientist,* February 12, 2011.

20. Source: National Vital Statistics Reports, Vol. 58, No. 14, March 31, 2010.

21. See "The Ways to Happiness."

22. S. Hodge and M. Boord, *The Illustrated Tibetan Book of the Dead: A New Translation with Commentary* (New York: Sterling Publishing, 1999).

23. That's how it looks in Belgium. A 2002 law allows an exception in the penal code from the established legal prohibition of killing. According to the law, assisted suicide is not subject to prosecution if an adult, terminally ill, conscious patient expressed the wish for life-ending provisions in front of multiple witnesses. A month must pass between the wish for assisted suicide and life-ending measures.

24. Source: Organ Procurement and Transplantation Network. June 1, 2012. http://optn.transplant.hrsa.gov (only donations from deceased).

25. Tissue donations include cornea, bones, etc.

26. P. Pearsall, *The Heart's Code* (New York: Broadway Books, 1998).

27. See "Rebirth in the Realms of Existence."

28. Photo by Thomas L. Kelly.

29. Lopön Tsechu Rinpoche, "The Intermediate States," part 3, "The Bardo of Clear Light," in *Buddhism Today*, 10 (2001), 9.

30. See "Preparation for Death."

31. Ole Nydahl, *Riding the Tiger* (Blue Dolphin Publishing, 1992) and "Conscious Dying."

32. See "Conscious Dying."

33. The old tantras had already been destroyed by the shamans in 800 AD.

34. Detailed explanations can be found from my teacher Tenga Rinpoche, from whom I and others received the Shitro-initiation several times. See Tenga Rinpoche, *Übergang und Befreiung*, 1996.

35. The precise chronological process depends on one's personal karma and can also be considerably shorter.

36. See "The Crucial Moment."

37. Milarepa was one of the most famous Tibetan accomplishers, the main disciple of Marpa and the teacher of Gampopa.

Because of his unshakable trust in his teacher and his will to meditate even in the most difficult conditions, he achieved complete realization in one life.

38. Photo by Ginger Neumann.

39. See fig. Fortunate Moments for Phowa for Others.

40. Status 2010.

41. See "The Ways to Happiness," "Refuge."

42. Photo by David Bauke.

43. Source: News Agency RUFO, December 4, 2004.

44. In my books *Entering the Diamond Way* and *Riding the Tiger,* the importance of Kalu Rinpoche becomes very apparent.

45. A so-called *ku-dung.*

46. We got the confirmation of the following chronicle by the caretaking doctor Mitchell Levy, Ph.D., through many Tibetan friends. See R. Ray, *Secret of the Vajra World* (Boston: Shambhala, 2001), p. 465-480.

47. See "The Crucial Moment."

Glossary

accomplisher (male, female: Skt. *yogi, yogini,* Tib. *naljorpa, naljorma*): Buddhist practitioner who focuses mainly on realizing the nature of mind, independent of outer securities or societal conventions. In Asia Buddhists were monks, lay practitioners, or yogis. Today, because of the good general education in the West, the lifestyles and views of lay practitioners and of yogis have become more intermingled.

appearance (Tib. *nang*): At the end of the dying process the white male energy from the seed of the father, which rests on the highest point of the head during life, moves down in the center of the body towards the heart level, while thirty-three kinds of anger and hatred dissolve.

attainment (Tib. *thob*): Approximately twenty to thirty minutes after clinical death, after the white male energy (appearance) and the red female energy (increase) have met at heart level, seven veils of ignorance dissolve, and for one instant everything becomes black and quiet.

bardo (Tib. literally: "between two," *Skt. antarābhava*): Generally, any intermediate state or transition. In the teachings of the Diamond Way, four or six bardos are usually mentioned. In the

West most people understand it as the time between death and the next rebirth.

bardo of becoming (Skt. *bhāvāntarābhava,* Tib. *sipai bardo*): The time from about the tenth day after death until conception.

bardo of death: The time from the beginning of the irreversible process of dying until rebirth. This phase is usually referred to simply as the bardo in the West.

bardo of dream (Skt. *svapanāntarābhava,* Tib. *milam bardo*): The time of the inwardly directed senses during sleep and (mainly unaware) dreams. Takes place within the bardo of life.

bardo of dying (Skt. *mumūrsāntarābhava,* Tib. *chikai bardo*): The time between the first indication of dying and about thirty minutes after the last breath. The bardo of dying takes place within the bardo of death.

bardo of life (Skt. *jatyantarābhava,* Tib. *rangzin bardo*): The time between conception and the beginning of dying.

bardo of meditation (Skt. *samādhyantarābhava,* Tib. *samtan bardo*): The time of the real state of absorption during meditation. Takes place within the bardo of life.

bardo of suchness (Skt. *dharmatāntarābhava,* Tib. *chönyi bardo*): The time from the actual moment of death as it is understood in Buddhism—i.e. from the end of the bardo of dying—until about ten days afterwards. Also known as the bardo of the ultimate nature, or the bardo of dharmata.

Bardo Thödröl: The name of the Tibetan text known in the West as *The Tibetan Book of the Dead*. Literally, "liberation through listening in the intermediate state."

basic thoughts: See Four Basic Thoughts.

bell (Skt. *ghanta,* Tib. *trilbu*): A ritual object used together with a dorje, symbolizing wisdom and space, respectively. On the level of the Diamond Way, the bell and dorje together denote the inseparability of space (female) and joy (male), of wisdom and compassion.

bindu: See thigle.

Black Coat (Tib. *Bernagchen*): The main protector of the Karma Kagyü lineage. Black-blue in color, he is shown either jumping or with his consort Radiant Goddess (Tib. *Palden Lhamo*), riding on a mule. In his right hand he holds a chopping knife that cuts through all hindrances, in his left hand a skull bowl with the heart's blood of the ego.

Black Crown: The special attribute of the Karmapas. In the moment of his enlightenment, Karmapa received the Black Crown, woven from the wisdom hair of the dakinis, who crowned him "Master of buddha activity" with it. The crown is a power-field that is constantly above Karmapa's head and is visible to highly accomplished beings. During the Crown

Ceremony he uses a replica of this crown. Seeing or meditating on the Black Crown causes an openness that allows one to purify the deepest levels of mind and to realize its nature.

blessing: According to the Tibetan texts, blessing is a strong method to transmit spiritual and mental maturity. This is made possible through the equality of space and bliss everywhere and the buddha nature that is inherent in everyone. In the Diamond Way the teacher is able to transmit an insight into the nature of mind through the enthusiasm and openness of his students, and thus give them a taste of their inherent possibilities and a deep trust in their own development.

bodhicitta (Skt., Tib. *changchub kyi sem*): See enlightened mind.

bodhisattva (Skt., Tib. *changchub sem pa*): Somebody who strives for enlightenment for the benefit of all beings without ever losing courage. This attitude corresponds to the ideal of the Great Way, to which the attitude in the Diamond Way also belongs. On the one hand, a bodhisattva is somebody who has understood emptiness and has developed compassion; on the other hand, this term is used for those who have taken the Bodhisattva Promise.

Bodhisattva Promise: The promise to accomplish buddha-hood for the benefit of all beings and to work with diligence and strength until all beings are liberated or enlightened. It is taken in the presence of a realized bodhisattva and is repeated in the context of daily meditation to strengthen this attitude.

bond, bonds (Skt. *samaya*, Tib. *damtsig*): The basis for fast spiritual growth in Diamond Way Buddhism. Through the unbroken bond to the lama, to the buddha aspects, and to those with whom one has received empowerments and teachings, the practitioner quickly develops his inherent qualities.

buddha (Skt., Tib. *sangye*): A name for the enlightened state of mind. In Tibetan, "sang" means "completely purified" of all veils that cloud the clarity of mind, and "gye" means "complete development" of all inherent qualities of mind. These inherent qualities are mainly fearlessness, unending joy, unlimited compassion, wisdom, and activity for the good of all beings. The Buddha of our time is the historical Buddha Shakyamuni, the fourth of one thousand historical buddhas who will manifest in this eon. Each historical Buddha introduces a new period of dharma.

buddha activities, also Four Buddha Activities: They describe compassionate, spontaneous and effortless behavior, the ability to do the right thing at the right place in the right time. There are four buddha activities: the pacifying, increasing, fascinating, and powerfully protecting actions of a buddha. The basis for these activities is the ability to rest in that which is.

buddha forms, buddha aspects (Skt. *deva or ishtadeva*, Tib. *yidam*): One of the Three Roots. The limitless qualities of the enlightened mind express themselves through these countless light and energy forms. By identifying with them in meditation and in everyday life, they awaken the buddha nature, which is inherent in everyone. They are seen as inseparable from one's own teacher. In order to be able to meditate on them, one needs the permission of, or an empowerment from, a lama who holds the appropriate transmission.

buddhahood: See enlightenment.   .

buddha nature: The nature of mind; the potential of buddhahood that is inherent in all beings.

Buddha of Limitless Life (Skt. *Amitayus,* Tib. *Tsepame*): Emanation of the Buddha of Limitless Light in the Joy State, embodying long life and health. He is of red color, sits in the lotus posture, and holds a vase with the nectar of long life in his hands, which are joined together in the gesture of meditation. An empowerment into him can be life-prolonging, along with a favorable karma.

Buddha of Limitless Light (Skt. *Amitabha,* Tib. *Öpame*): Buddha of discriminating wisdom, ruby-colored and sitting. His hands rest in his lap and hold a bowl with the nectar of highest accomplishment. His realm of consciousness is the Pure Land of Highest Joy (Dewachen), which beings with strong wishes are able to reach thanks to this buddha's previous promises.

central channel (Skt. *avādhuti,* Tib. *uma*): The energy axis in the center of the body. It arises through movement of the white energy (from the sperm) of the father upwards and the red energy (from the egg) of the mother downwards and is completely developed twenty-nine days after fertilization. It starts at the highest point of the skull and ends in the shape of a test tube four finger-widths below the navel in the center of the body. The moment when both energies meet during dying is considered the moment of death from a Buddhist perspective.

chakra (Skt., Tib. *khorlo*): Five power wheels or energy wheels along the central channel with branching energy spokes in the center of the body. The head chakra (with thirty-two spokes) controls the body, the throat chakra (sixteen) the speech, the heart chakra (eight) is responsible for the mind and the unhindered access to space, the navel chakra (sixty-four) for fantasy and creativity, and the secret chakra (thirty-two), which is located four fingers below the navel in the center of the body, for vitality and sexual energy.

Chöd (Tib. literally: "cutting through"): An advanced yidam meditation that has the goal of cutting through the ego-illusion.

chödral: See tudam.

chönyi bardo (Tib.): The experience of the dharmata or intermediate state of suchness; an experience of the truth space that one is able to reach from a very high level of development exactly at the moment of death; corresponds to the experience of the Truth State.

clarity (Skt. *vyakta*, Tib. *sälwa*): Emptiness, clarity, and limitlessness are absolute qualities of mind, which cannot be separated from one another. Clarity is mind's inherent ability to experience without interruption. Its realization is the manifestation of the Joy State of enlightenment.

Clear Light: Experience of emptiness, in which space and appearance become one.

Conscious Dying: See Phowa.

Crown Ceremony: During the life of the 5th Karmapa, the Chinese emperor had a replica made of the Black Crown. Since that time the Karmapas have shown them during Crown Ceremonies while they rest in deep meditation at the same time. The 16th Karmapa is considered to be an emanation of "Almighty Ocean." The Black Crown belongs to the treasures of the Karma Kagyü lineage.

detong (Tib.): The experience of emptiness as being blissful; a view of the Kagyü and Nyingma accomplishers belonging to the Buddhist tantras.

Dewachen: See Pure Land of Highest Joy.

dharma (Skt., Tib. *chö*): Buddha's teachings. Part of the Buddhist refuge. It is structured in different ways, often into Theravada, Mahayana, and Vajrayana, the three levels of teaching that the Buddha gave to his students according to their different attitudes.

Diamond Dagger (Skt. *Vajrakilaya*, Tib. *Dorje Phurba*): Powerfully protective emanation of Diamond Mind;

overcomes all hindrances, especially to meditation.

Diamond in Hand (Skt. *Vajrapani,* Tib. *Channa Dorje*): One of the three best known bodhisattvas besides Wisdom Buddha and Loving Eyes; stands for powerful activity and endurance.

Diamond Mind (Skt. *Vajrasattva,* Tib. *Dorje Sempa*): The buddha who represents the purifying power of all buddhas. He is depicted as white and sitting. His right hand holds a dorje to his heart and the left one a bell at his hip. He is the Joy State of Buddha Akshobya.

Diamond Way (Skt. *Vajrayana,* Tib. *Dorje Thegpa*): Also called Tantrayana and Mantrayana. The highest level of Buddha's teachings, encompassing body, speech, and mind with the goal of full enlightenment. In this practice, the goal also becomes the path by using fast and profound methods. These teachings can only be used with the perspective of seeing everything as fundamentally pure.

diamond: See dorje.

djalü (Tib.): See rainbow body.

dorje (Skt., Tib. *vajra,* literally: "king of stones, diamond"): A symbol of indestructibility and stability that characterizes the highest state of mind, enlightenment. Ritual object that symbolizes the methods of the Diamond Way as well as compassion and joy. See also bell.

elements: All beings emerge out of the five elements: earth (everything solid); water (everything fluent); fire (everything that gives off heat); wind (everything that gives movement); and, space (encompasses all possibilities). During the process of dying all elements dissolve successively again into space.

Emanation State (Skt. *nirmanakaya,* Tib. *tulku*): See tulku.

emptiness (Skt. *shunyata,* Tib. *tong panyi*): Empty of independent existence, nothing arises by itself, but rather is dependent upon conditions. Emptiness is the ultimate nature of all outer and inner phenomena and cannot be grasped through concepts.

energy channel (Skt. *nadi,* Tib. *tsa*): See energy system.

energy drop (Skt. *bindu, tilaka,* Tib. *thigle*): See thigle and energy system.

energy system: The different energy distributions that are necessary when a child comes into existence, influence all physical and mental functions, and dissolve again during the process of dying; the complete system consists of the central channel, two side channels, five chakras and 72,000 buddha energies. See also nadi, pranas, bindus, thigle.

energy wind (Skt. *prana, vayu,* Tib. *lung*): See energy system.

energy awareness: The connection between life energy and consciousness.

enlightened mind (Skt. *bodhicitta,* Tib. *chang chub kyi sem*): The wish to reach enlightenment for the good of all beings, and the basis for the Great Way and the Diamond Way. The enlightened mind has two aspects: the conditioned or relative, and the absolute or ultimate. In the conditioned aspect, the enlightened mind consists of the wish to benefit all beings, accompanied by perfecting oneself through the Six Liberating Actions. The ultimate or absolute enlightened mind recognizes the inseparability of emptiness and compassion. This leads to spontaneous and effortless activity which is beyond any concept or hesitation, as subject, object and action are no longer experienced as separate from one another. The enlightened mind is the attitude of a bodhisattva, the enlightened attitude.

enlightenment/enlightened: See buddha.

Essence State (Skt. *svabhavikakaya,* Tib. *ngowonyiku*): One of the Four Buddha States. The three states Truth State, Joy State, and Emanation State together express the Essence State.

experiencer: The ability and quality of mind to be aware even if there are no objects of perception. It is not realized at all by most people.

Form States (Skt. *rupakaya*): The Joy State and the Emanation State. They arise from the Truth State and bring benefit for others.

Foundational Practices (Tib. *chagchen ngöndro*): The preparation for the Great Seal. Also called the Four Special

Preliminaries. With the Foundational Practices one creates count-less good impressions in the subconscious. With each of these practices, there are 111,111 repetitions. These meditations are:
- taking refuge and developing the enlightened attitude through prostrations;
- purifying the impressions that bring suffering through the Diamond Mind meditation;
- offering good impressions with Mandala Offerings; and,
- Meditation on the Lama (Guru Yoga).

Four Basic Thoughts: Also called the Four Ordinary Prelimi-naries. Four thoughts that develop a deep understanding of the basic facts of our lives and direct mind towards the dharma. These thoughts are:
- The precious opportunity in our current existence to encounter the teachings which lead to liberation and enlightenment.
- Impermanence: since all conditions are understood to be in constant change, one should use every opportunity to recognize mind.
- Karma, cause and effect: that one shapes one's life with one's thoughts, words and actions.
- The disadvantages of conditioned existence; enlightenment as the only true and lasting joy.

Four Foundational practices: See Foundational Practices.

four main schools or lineages of Tibetan Buddhism: Kagyü (Tib. literally: oral transmission), Nyingma (Tib. literally: old style), Sakya (a region in Tibet), Gelug (Tib. virtue tradition or Ganden tradition).

Gelug lineage/school, Gelugpas (Tib. two possible translations: the Ganden School, named after their main monastery,
or the Virtuous School): Also called the "Yellow Hat" School;
the newest of the four main lineages of Tibetan Buddhism. This
reformed school, first founded in the 14th century by Tsongkhapa, emphasizes the textual studies as well as the monastic
tradition. Although this school also possesses various tantric
transmissions, they see themselves mainly as Great Way rather
than Diamond Way.

gomlung: See transmission through meditation.

Great Perfection (Skt. *Maha Ati,* Tib. *Dzogchen, Dzogpa
Chenpo*): The ultimate teaching of the Nyingma or Old School.
Its essence and goal correspond to the Great Seal of the Kagyü
transmission. However, the methods and path are different.

Great Seal (Skt. *Mahamudra,* Tib. *Chagchen, Chagya Chenpo*):
The Great Seal of realization. Buddha promised that this is the
ultimate teaching. It is mainly taught in the Kagyü school and
leads to a direct experience of the nature of mind. The Great Seal
encompasses the basis, way, and goal. With trust in one's buddha
nature, one tries to rest in the inseparability of the experiencer,
that which is being experienced, and the experience itself. As a
result, mind recognizes itself and seals its enlightenment.

Great Way (Skt. *Mahayana,* Tib. *Thegchen*): The way of the bodhisattvas, where one strives for enlightenment for the benefit of

all beings. Compassion and wisdom are deepened through study, analysis, and meditation over a long time, and then expand into insight. The Great Way sometimes is used synonymously with the term sutra.

guru yoga (Skt., Tib. *lami naljor*): Meditation on the teacher (lama) as the essence of all buddhas. Through this practice, just as in an empowerment, one receives the blessing of the lama's body, speech and mind, and the Four Buddha States are awakened. In the practice, one melts together and identifies with the enlightened essence of the lama.

Highest Joy, also Buddha of Highest Joy (Skt. *Chakrasamvara*, literally: "Wheel of Highest Bliss," Tib. *Korlo Demchok*): The buddha of radiant and impersonal joy that is the true nature of our mind. He is deep blue, standing, with hands crossed at heart level and holding a dorje and bell, with an inspiring appearance that transforms attachment. Often in union with Red Wisdom; important meditation form in the Karma Kagyü lineage.

Hinayana: See Small Way.

increase (Tib. *ched*): The red female energy, which dwells four fingers below the navel in the center of the body during life, moves towards the heart level after appearance, while forty different kinds of attachment dissolve.

empowerment (Skt. *abhisheka*, Tib. *wang*): Also called initiation. The introduction of a practitioner into the power-field of a buddha form, most often connected with ceremonies where a student receives an empowerment to meditate on that form. Practice empowerments are connected with promises. Empowerments can also be given as blessings, also called permission empowerments. Here one makes a bond with the lama, and obstacles on the way to enlightenment are purified. For Diamond Way practice, the oral transmission (Tib. *lung*) and instructions (Tib. *tri*) are necessary, along with the empowerment. The more immediate way of a guided meditation in one's own language (Tib. *gomlung*) accomplishes the same goals. In the Kagyü lineage, meditation on the teacher (guru yoga) is the most important. All buddha forms are experienced as inseparable from the teacher.

intermediate state: See bardo.

Joy State (Skt. *sambhogakaya,* Tib. *long ku*): The body of perfect enjoyment, one of the Four Buddha States. The enlightened expression of the clarity of mind, its free play, and the experience of highest joy. This state is experienced when mind recognizes its rich possibilities on the level of fearlessness. It manifests from the Truth State as various buddha forms and their power-fields. Advanced bodhisattvas can encounter these forms and receive blessings as well as direct insight. See also tulku.

joy level: See Joy State.

Kagyü lineage/school, Kagyüpas: The accomplisher transmission within the four main schools of Tibetan Buddhism. Encompasses the old (Tib. *Nyingma*) and new (Tib. *Sarma*) teachings that reached Tibet. Being heavily practice-oriented, it is sometimes called the "oral" or "perfecting" school. It was brought to Tibet around 1050 by the hero Marpa and draws its strength from the close relationship between teacher and student. Four major and eight minor schools have their origin in the four main students of Gampopa. Major and minor relate to the direct connection to Gampopa (major or main schools) or indirect connection through a student of Gampopa (minor or subsidiary schools). Today, out of the major schools, only the Karma Kagyü, whose spiritual leader is the Karmapa, remains. From the eight minor schools, the Drugpa and Drikung Kagyü have many supporters in Bhutan and Ladakh.

Kalachakra calendar: A calendar starting in the year 1027, with a sixty-year cycle as its basis. One month lasts from one new moon until the next. All components, from a single day to a sixty-year cycle, are strictly mathematically predefined.

Kangyur (Tib.): Translation of the Buddha's words. A collection of the direct teachings of the Buddha—in 100, 103, 106, or 108 volumes, depending on the edition. See also Tenjur.

karma (Skt., Tib. *ley*): Literally: action; the law of cause and effect, according to which one experiences the world in correspondence to the impressions stored in mind, created through one's actions of body, speech and mind. This means that one decides one's own future with one's present actions.

Karma Kagyü (-school, -lineage): See Kagyü (-school/-lineage)

.

ku-dung: Mummified body of a high accomplisher who has died in the posture of meditation.

lama (Tib. literally, "highest principle," Skt. *guru*): One of the Three Roots. Buddhist teacher, especially important in the Diamond Way as he is the key to the deepest teachings. In the guru yoga meditation on the lama, one receives his blessing, through which one may momentarily experience the true nature of mind. The lama mirrors the Three States of Enlightenment.

lhaktong (Tib., Skt. *vipashyana*): Insight meditation. This meditation practice is used as a method in the Sutra way as well as in the Tantra way and builds on a stable calm-abiding experience (Skt. *shamatha*, Tib. *shinay*). One tries to maintain from moment to moment the view of the non-duality of perceiving consciousness and perceived objects. There is an analytical and a direct approach.

liberating actions: See Six Liberating Actions.

liberation: Release from the cycle of existence (Skt. *samsara*); the state of mind in which all suffering and the causes for suffering are completely overcome. It happens through dissolving the false idea of a presumed "I." On this level all disturbing emotions fall away. When the last stiff concepts are also let go, one becomes enlightened.

Limitless Life: See Buddha of Limitless Life.

long-life empowerment: An empowerment into the power-field of a buddha, like Lady of Long Life, White Liberatrice or Limitless Light, who have chosen to work to prolong life. These empowerments are very effective and in great demand. See also Buddha of Limitless Life.

lotus posture: A meditation posture, also known as the full lotus, in which the legs are crossed, corresponding to the form of a lotus blossom. Sitting in this manner, the right foot rests on the left thigh near the groin, and the left foot rests on the right thigh. The soles of the feet are face up. In half lotus, the right leg rests on the left.

Loving Eyes (Skt. *Avalokiteshvara,* Tib. *Chenrezig*): The buddha of compassion and of non-discriminating love. He is in the Joy State, white in color, seated in full meditation posture. He has four arms. His outer right hand holds a crystal mala, which frees all beings from the conditioned world. His middle hands hold the jewel of enlightenment in front of his heart. His outer left hand holds a lotus blossom, which shows the purity of his view. His eyes see all beings.

lung (Tib., Skt. *agama*): Ritual reading or recitation of Diamond Way texts. Simply hearing the syllables transmits their inner meaning. See also empowerment.

Mahakala (Skt., Tib. *Nagpo Chenpo*): Great Black One. A category of protectors, of which the two-armed form is known as Bernagchen. See also Black Coat.

Mahayana: See Great Way.

mala: String of prayer beads consisting of 108 beads; used, among other things, to count mantras during meditation.

mandala (Skt., Tib. *khyilkhor*, literally: center and surroundings): A pure mandala is the power-field of a buddha that emerges out of the countless possibilities of space or the depiction thereof; it is always free of an ego-illusion and is, therefore, a liberated state of consciousness free of disturbing emotions. An impure mandala determines to a great extent the behavior of beings. It appears because every unenlightened being thinks, against all logic, that there is something permanent or really existing which can be called an "I," around which everything circles.

mantra (Skt., Tib. *ngag*): Natural vibration of a buddha aspect; activates the Buddha aspect's power-field. Many Diamond Way meditations have a phase where mantras are repeated.

meditation (Skt. *bhāvanā or sadhana,* Tib. *gom*): The Tibetan word gom means "become familiar with" and expresses a process in which mind tries to let go of its veils. For this, one uses methods that bring what is understood intellectually into one's own experience. On the highest level, meditation means to effortlessly remain in that which is. On the various levels of Buddha's teachings, different methods are taught, but they can be summarized essentially as calm-abiding and insight. In the Diamond Way, the most important methods are identification with enlightenment, awakening the enlightened power-field using mantras, gratitude, and holding the pure view. Just as it was earlier in Tibet, in the caves of the accomplishers, so today in the West, guided meditation (Tib. *gomlung*) enables a large number of people to gain access to the countless methods of the Diamond Way.

meditation on the 16th Karmapa: This meditation was given by the 16th Karmapa. It is a form of guru yoga and is used in the Diamond Way Buddhist centers of the Karma Kagyü lineage as the main practice for public meditation sessions.

meditation schools of Tibet: See Gelug, Kagyü, Nyingma, and Sakya.

Middle Way (of emptiness; Skt. *Madhyamaka*, Tib. *Uma Chenpo*): Literally "not even the center"; a precise conceptual analysis of all phenomena in order to recognize them as not being ultimately real or existing. Subdivided into rangtong- (empty in itself) and shentong—(empty of something else) Madhyamaka.

mind: Experienced as the habitual stream of clear and conscious experiencing. In its unenlightened state it expresses its ability to think, perceive, and remember through the consciousness. Its true enlightened nature is free of any self-centeredness and perceives itself as not separate from space—as indestructible, limitless awareness. The recognition of its nature leads to fearlessness, self-arisen love, and active compassion.

nadis (Skt., Tib. *tsa*): Energy channels. Form the energy system, along with the energy winds or movements (pranas), and essence of the physical body or energy drops (bindus).

nature of mind: See buddha nature.

NDE: Near-Death Experience. Mentioned for the first time during ancient Greek civilization. The experiences during the first minutes after clinical death or the descending of the white energy of the father toward the heart. Current scientific research is being carried out by, among others, Dr. Pim van Lommel, M.D. (NL), Dr. Peter Fenwick, M.D. (USA) and Dr. Sam Parnia, M.D. (GB).

Ngöndro (Tib.): See Foundational Practices.

nirvana (Skt., Tib. *nyang ngen le depa*): Generally, liberation from suffering in samsara; especially in the Mahayana it is a state of perfection (buddhahood).

Nyingma lineage/school, Nyingmapas: The oldest of the four main lineages of Tibetan Buddhism, "the old school." It was founded in the eighth century by the Indian master Guru Rinpoche (Tib., Skt. *Padmasambhava*). There is a distinction between the Kama tradition (the school of direct transmission from teacher to student, which goes all the way back to Buddha Shakyamuni) and the Terma tradition, the transmission of hidden "treasures" which were rediscovered and propagated later. In the year 800, King Langdarma turned against Buddhism and destroyed these transmission lineages. But the tertöns (treasure finders) rediscovered the teachings of Guru Rinpoche for us today. Many *tertons* were Kagyüs, and were together with women. In sharing the transmissions, a close connection developed between the Kagyü and the Nyingma schools.

paramitas: See liberating actions.

phases of meditation:
- building-up phase (Tib. *kyerim*): one calls to mind a buddha aspect
- mantra phase: one repeats a mantra
- melting phase (Tib. *dzogrim*): everything becomes awareness and one rests in it

Phowa *(*Tib., Skt. *samkrānti):* A practice of the Diamond Way with which one prepares for the moment of death.

Phowa for others (hook of compassion): A practice with which one can help relatives or close friends in death (except during the sixty-eight hours of unconsciousness) get to the Pure Land of Highest Joy, until the forty-ninth day after death.

Phowa into the Emanation State (*Nirmanakaya-Phowa*): The possibility to reach the power-field of Great Joy, available from the tenth to the forty-ninth day after death, if one has deeply internalized and lived four attitudes relating to this pure land: one has the wish to be born there; one has a clear imagination of the Buddha; one avoids harmful actions, and wants to reach enlightenment for the benefit of all beings.

Phowa into the Joy State (*Sambhogakaya-Phowa*): The possibility to reach liberation from about 68 hours after death until the tenth day. One experiences phenomena either as the light forms of the buddhas or the lamas or as illusions; one is able to achieve it if one has experienced the dream-like nature of phenomena in meditation and the richness of all phenomena during the building-up or mantra phase.

Phowa into the Truth State (*Dharmakaya-Phowa*): The opportunity to achieve the Truth State that occurs twenty to thirty minutes after the last breathing-out using the methods of *tudam* or *chödral* (to hold mind in the heart), *djalü* (rainbow body) or the "breathing-out-into-space"; one is able to achieve it if one dwells in the state of naked awareness during the melting phase of meditation.

Phowa of blessing (for oneself): The meditation of Conscious Dying. One learns to send the consciousness out of one's body into the heart center of the Buddha of Limitless Light and thus prepares oneself for later death. The effect of a successful practice is to have less fear and to go to the Pure Land of Highest Joy while dying. From there, one can develop until enlightenment and be reborn to help other beings.

power-field: See mandala.

pranas (Skt., Tib. *lung*): Energy winds or movements. Make up the energy system, along with the energy channels (nadis), and essence of the physical body or energy drops (bindus).

protectors (Skt. *dharmapala*, Tib. *chökyong or gönpo*): One of the Three Roots; they remove obstacles on the path to enlightenment and make every experience into a step on the way. Protectors, the source of buddha activity, are, along with the yidams, expressions of the Joy State and are essentially inseparable from the lama. In the Kagyü lineage, Black Coat (Skt. *Mahakala,* Tib. *Bernagchen*) and Radiant Goddess (Skt. *Shri Devi,* Tib. *Palden Lhamo*) are the most important protectors.

Pure Land of Highest Joy (Skt. *Sukhavati,* Tib. *Dewachen*): The pure land of the Buddha of Limitless Light. It is particularly easy to reach through practices on the Buddha of Limitless Light and Phowa.

pure land: The power-field of a buddha; a beyond-personal, unconditioned, joyful state of mind in which all conditions for Buddhist practice for realization and enlightenment exist, and great merit can be accumulated. The most well-known Pure Land is The Pure Land of Highest Joy (*Dewachen*) of the Buddha of Limitless Light. See also Phowa.

pure power-field of a Buddha: See mandala.

pure view: The view kept in the Diamond Way: one practices seeing the world and all beings as the self-liberating play of space.

rainbow body (Tib. *djalü*): Highly realized masters are able to transform their body into energy during the process of dying; only physical parts that do not have nerves (e.g. hair, finger and toe-nails) remain. See also Phowa into the Truth State.

rangtong (Tib.): "Empty in itself." The view of emptiness in which neither an "I" nor any phenomena have their own nature, held mainly by the Gelugpas.

realms of existence, six: Six levels of consciousness in which one can be reborn. They are the three realms of conditioned happiness: the god-realm, demigod realm, and the realm of human beings, and the three realms of suffering: the animal realm, realm of hungry ghosts, and the hell realms.

Red Buddha: see Buddha of Limitless Light.

Red Hat lineages: See Kagyü, Nyingma, Sakya.

Red Wisdom (Skt. *Vajravarahi,* Tib. *Dorje Pamo*): Female buddha aspect embodying the ultimate highest wisdom of all buddhas. Red in color and in dancing posture, she holds a chopping knife with her raised right hand, with which she cuts through everything petty, while her left hand holds a skull bowl with the nectar of liberation. She is an important meditation form of the Kagyü lineage and, in union with Highest Bliss (Tib. *Demchok*), is the most important Kagyü yidam.

retreat: A period of meditating for days, weeks or years in a quiet and isolated place, not being distracted by the entanglements of life; most effective if one has a clear goal and a daily schedule, under the guidance of a Buddhist teacher. There are open and closed retreats for individuals, couples and groups. Times of withdrawal create more distance from the experiences of everyday life and deepen meditation experience.

rinpoche (Tib. literally: "precious one"): A title of respect, often given to Buddhist lamas.

Sakya lineage/school, Sakyapas: One of the four main schools of Tibetan Buddhism, founded by Khön Könchok Gyalpo in the eleventh century; in this school weight is given to both intellectual study and meditation practice.

samsara (Skt., Tib. *khorwa*): The cycle of existence; involuntary reincarnation in conditioned states.

sangha (Skt., Tib. *gendün*): The community of practitioners, often used to designate a Buddhist group; as part of Buddhist refuge, it indicates the realized friends on the way.

shentong (Tib.): "Empty of others." The view of emptiness held generally by the Kagyü, Sakya and Nyingma lineages. It means empty of all superficial veils. Basic awareness experiences emptiness, but is itself not a "thing"; is also called The Great Middle Way (Skt. *Maha Madhyamaka*, Tib. *Uma Chenpo*).

shinay (Tib., Skt. *shamatha*): A meditation method also called tranquil mind or calm-abiding; while meditating on an actual, imagined or abstract object, one practices letting the mind be one-pointed and dwell without distraction. In both Sutra and Tantra, shinay is the foundation for recognizing the true nature of mind.

shitro empowerment: a Nyingma transmission into the 42

peaceful and 58 powerfully protecting Buddhas who have their seat in the heart or head chakra.

side channels: Part of the energy system; they are the left channel (Skt. *lalana*, Tib. *kyangma*) and right channel (Skt. *rasana*, Tib. *roma*).

Six Liberating Actions (Skt. *paramitas*, Tib. *parol tu jinpa druk*): Liberating actions of the bodhisattvas; most often the following six are mentioned: generosity, vast and conscious action, patience, joyful effort, meditation, and liberating wisdom.

Six Teachings of Naropa (Tib. *naro chö druk*): Very effective methods of the Kagyü lineage, only practiced in retreat; their goal is the recognition of the nature of mind by means of its energy aspects. They include the following meditations: Inner Heat (Skt. *chandali*, Tib. *tummo*), Clear Light (Skt. *prabhabhava*, Tib. *ösel*), Dream Yoga (Skt. *svapnadarshana*, Tib. *milam*), Illusory Body (Skt. *mayakaya*, Tib. *gyulu*), Intermediate State (Skt. *antarabhava*, Tib. *bardo*) and Transference of Consciousness or Conscious Dying (Skt. *samkrānti*, Tib. *phowa*).

Small Way (Skt. *Hinayana*, today *Theravada* or Foundational Vehicle, Tib. *Theg Chung*): The way of the arhats or listeners (Skt. *shravakas*, Tib. *nyenthö*) and individual buddhas or solitary realizers (Skt. *pratyekabuddhas*, Tib. *rang sangye*); here the focus is on one's own liberation.

space: Timeless and present everywhere as the inherent potential of mind in everything. It contains knowledge, experiences joy,

joy, and expresses itself as meaningful and loving. Constantly realizing this space in and around oneself is full enlightenment. It is often misunderstood as nothingness, something missing, or a black hole. However, it connects everything. Described by Buddha as emptiness, space encompasses and recognizes all times and directions.

store consciousness (also base consciousness or Skt. *alaya vijnana*): A function of mind that stores all impressions and lets them mature again with the appearance of corresponding conditions, and manifest in the outer world; it colors one's experience, and through karma is the basis for the next rebirth.

stupa (Skt., Tib. *chörten*): A form, often a construction, which symbolizes perfect enlightenment, usually filled with relics and written mantras; translated from the Tibetan, *chör* means gifts and *ten* means foundation for offering gifts (of body, speech and mind) to enlightenment. Buddha gave teachings on stupas in the Sutra of Dependent Arising. It represents the transformation of all emotions and elements into the five wisdoms and the Five Buddha Families. It is used by Buddhists as a site for making beyond-personal wishes for the benefit of all beings and is circumambulated in clockwise direction. Often used as symbol representing the sangha.

Sutra (Skt., Tib. *do*): Often called the Causal Way; on this path one establishes, over a long time, the causes for enlightenment in order to recognize the characteristic of all things, their emptiness. In its further meaning, literally "guideline," it is a term for the individual specific discourses of Buddha. See also Great Way.

Tantra, Buddhist (Skt.): A highly effective part of the Great Way in which identification with enlightenment and holding the Pure View are the most important methods; Tantrayana (the Tantra path) has the same meaning as Vajrayana (Skt., *Diamond Way*) and Mantrayana (the Mantra path). The goal, buddhahood, becomes the way. A fast way to enlightenment, but one that implies trust in one's own mind and a compassionate attitude.

Tengyur (Tib.): The collection of the commentaries of the Indian masters on the teachings of the Buddha (*Kangyur*), between 225 and 256 volumes, depending on the edition.

thangka (Tib.): A scroll painting on which different buddha aspects are depicted; they serve as a support for meditation.

Theravada: "Way of the Elders of the (Religious) Order." See also Small Way.

thigle (Tib., Skt. *bindu or tilaka*): Essence of the energy; encompasses the five elements and contains the vital energy. It arises during conception out of the central channel at heart level and follows the white father-essence upwards and the red mother-essence downwards and thus forms the central channel.

Three Jewels (Skt. *tri ratna*, Tib. *könchog sum*): The Buddha, dharma, and sangha. All Buddhists worldwide take refuge in them.

Three Old Schools of Tibet: See Kagyü, Nyingma, and Sakya.

Three Roots (Skt. *trimūla*, Tib. *tsa sum*): lama, yidam, and protector. Above and beyond the Three Jewels, they are the refuge in the Diamond Way and make a fast track to enlightenment possible. They are the source (or roots) of blessing, realization and protection.

transmission through meditation (Tib. *gomlung*): Guided meditation; a common way in which meditations are taught in Diamond Way Buddhist centers; a breakthrough in the transmission of Buddhism in the West.

Truth State (Skt. *dharmakaya;* literally: "body of phenomena," Tib. *chöku*): One of the Three States of Enlightenment; the Truth State is timeless enlightenment and, as such, the empty nature of mind. It is the foundation for the Joy State and the Emanation State. It is the ultimate nature of a Buddha, beyond all forms, characteristics and limits. Recognition of the Truth State is beneficial for oneself and yields absolute fearlessness, whereas the Joy State and the Emanation State are for the sake of others.

tudam (Tib.): "To hold the mind in one's heart." A kind of Phowa into the Truth State. After the death of a highly realized person, mind dwells in the state of suchness in the heart.

tulku (Tib., Skt. *Nirmanakaya*): one of the Three States of Enlightenment; also called Emanation State. It expresses the ability of mind to show itself unobstructed out of space. In its highest meaning, Nirmanakaya refers to an historical Buddha, a "perfect tulku." Further kinds of tulkus are the "expert tulkus" (who, for example, act for the benefit of others as healer, artist or scientist), and the "born tulkus" (who, for example, can also choose a birth as an animal to help beings). There are tulkus who can clearly recall former lives and others who can barely remember them at all. Tulkus show themselves in order to make the access to buddha nature possible for beings. Tulku literally means "illusory body": One is not the body, but rather one has it, and uses it for the benefit of beings.

Vairocana (Skt., Tib. *Namparnangdse*): The Radiant One; central Buddha of the Five Buddha Families. He stands for the transformation of ignorance into all-pervading wisdom or intuition.

Vajrayana (Skt.): See Diamond Way.

wisdoms, five: The five buddha wisdoms are the true essence of the disturbing emotions. Through the transformation of ordinary experience, anger is recognized as a mirror-like state, showing the way things are without adding or subtracting anything (mirror-like wisdom). Pride becomes the ability to see all things as richness (equalizing wisdom). Attachment transforms into the capacity to distinguish things in their details and in how they work together (discriminating wisdom). Jealousy transforms itself into the ability to connect experiences together as steps in a historical process (wisdom of experience), and ignorance becomes all-pervading insight (all-pervading wisdom).

yidam (Tib., Skt. *deva*): One of the Three Roots; source of enlightened qualities.

Biographical Notes

Atisha (982–1054): Lived in Tibet from 1042 and founded the Kadampa tradition, together with the translator Rinchen Sangpo (958–1055) and his main disciple Dromtonpa (1004–1065). The teaching later became the core of the Gelug tradition by Je Tsongkhapa (1357–1419). Atisha was the holder of three transmissions: the one of the "Vast Behavior" by Asanga, the one of the "Deep View" by Nagarjuna and the one of the "Blessing and the Practice" by Naropa. Atisha brought the "vessel" (the revival of outer monastic forms) as well as the Mahayana basis to Tibet. He translated many teachings of Buddha from Sanskrit into Tibetan.

Ayang Rinpoche (1941–): Born into a nomad family in Eastern Tibet. After his escape from Tibet, he established two monasteries in southern India. He is the holder of several transmissions of Phowa (Conscious Dying) and has taught this practice in many countries.

Dalai Lama: The present Dalai Lama Tenzin Gyatso (born in 1935) is the 14th rebirth of the Dalai Lamas. The title "Dalai Lama ," meaning "Ocean-like teacher" in Mongolian, was bestowed by the Mongolian ruler Altan Khan on the third Dalai Lama in 1578. Their lineage of rebirths goes back to Gendün Drub (1391–1474). Starting from his fifth rebirth he became the political head of Tibet, but never the head of all Buddhists.

Dilgo Khyentse Rinpoche (1910–1991): One of the greatest realized Buddhist masters of the Nyingma and Kagyü school of the twentieth century and brought into the Kagyü lineage the form of the Phowa now used in the West. He was respected as an outstanding poet, scholar and Dzogchen master. Dilgo Khyentse was one of the last of a generation of great masters who were still able to finish their education in Tibet. Many high-level Tibetan lamas, such as the 14th Dalai Lama, regarded him as their teacher. In addition, he had many students in the West.

Gampopa (1079–1153): Milarepa's main student and teacher of the first Karmapa, Dusum Khyenpa. The Buddha prophesied that Gampopa would spread the Dharma all across Tibet. He united the Kadampa school of Atisha with the way of the Great Seal (Mahamudra) of Milarepa. The monastic Kagyü transmission began with him.

Referring to one of his philosophical masterpieces, *The Jewel Ornament of Liberation*, he said that reading it would be the same as meeting him. This book explains the views and path of the Great Way and is an excellent introduction into the foundations of Buddhism.

Guru Rinpoche (Skt. *Padmasambhava*, literally: "the Lotus Born," Tib. *Pema Jungne*): Brought Buddhism, in particular the Diamond Way transmissions, to Tibet in the eighth century. He led an exciting life and performed innumerable miracles. With his termas and his prophecies of the tertöns, he founded the Nyingma lineage. He is also highly esteemed by the Kagyüs and the Sakyas.

(Goshir) Gyaltsab Rinpoche (1954–): One of the lineage-holders at the time of the 16th Karmapa. Together with Tai Situ Rinpoche, he turned to the Chinese-supported, political Karmapa Urgyen Trinley in 1992.

Hambo Lama (here the 12th Pandito Hambo Lama Dorzho Itigilow, 1852–1927): Buryatian lama, who preserved his body after his death through a special meditation. Today he is completely undecayed and can be visited in his datsan (monastery) near Ulan Ude in Siberia.

Jamgön Kongtrul Rinpoche (1954–1992): Considered to be the third rebirth of one of the greatest scholars and meditation masters of the Karma Kagyü lineage, Jamgön Kongtrul Lodrö Thaye. The third Jamgön Kongtrul Rinpoche (Lodrö Chökyi Senge) escaped as a child together with the 16th Karmapa out of Tibet, and was brought up and educated in the Rumtek monastery in Sikkim. As an adolescent, he accompanied the 16th Karmapa on several journeys to the West and later became very active himself as a dharma teacher in the West. In 1992, however, he died prematurely in a car accident in Northern India.

Kalu Rinpoche (1904–1989): Lineage holder of the Shangpa tradition. He became a retreat master for the traditional three-year retreats. He left Tibet at request of the 16th Karmapa in 1957. Starting in 1971 he often traveled to Europe, North America and Southeast Asia. Among other activities, he was the teacher of the 14th Shamarpa, 12th Tai Situpa, third Jamgön Kongtrul and Lama Ole and Hannah Nydahl.

Karmapa (Tib. literally: "One who carries out the buddha activity" or "Master of Buddha Activity"): The first consciously reborn lama of Tibet and spiritual leader of the Karma Kagyü lineage since the 12th century. The Karmapa embodies the activity of all buddhas and was predicted by Buddha Shakyamuni and Guru Rinpoche. Before their deaths, many Karmapas left a letter that described the exact circumstances of their next birth. Until today there have been seventeen incarnations.

(1) Düsum Khyenpa, 1110–1193

(2) Karma Pakshi, 1204–1283

(3) Rangjung Dorje, 1284–1339

(4) Rölpe Dorje, 1340–1383

(5) Deshin Shegpa, 1384–1415

(6) Tongwa Dönden, 1416–1453

(7) Chödrak Gyamtso, 1454–1506

(8) Mikyö Dorje, 1507–1554

(9) Wangchug Dorje, 1556–1603

(10) Chöying Dorje, 1604–1674

(11) Yeshe Dorje, 1676–1702

(12) Changchub Dorje, 1703–1732

(13) Düdül Dorje, 1733–1797

(14) Thegchog Dorje, 1798–1868

(15) Khakhyab Dorje, 1871–1922

(16) Rangjung Rigpe Dorje, 1924–1981

(17) Trinley Thaye Dorje, 1983–present.

Lopön Tsechu Rinpoche (1918–2003): Born in Bhutan; at the age of thirteen his family escaped to Nepal because of a plague. There he became a close student of the Drukpa master

Sherab Dorje Rinpoche, who was his uncle. His education included longer retreats in the caves of the Himalayas. In 1944 he met the 16th Karmapa and also became his student. Lopön Tsechu Rinpoche was a key figure of Buddhism in Nepal. He took care of the Buddhist tribes in the country, used a lot of energy to preserve the Buddhist places, supported Tibetan refugees and worked as a counselor for the royal families of Nepal and Bhutan. Starting in 1987, Lopön Tsechu more frequently traveled with Lama Ole and Hannah Nydahl (having been their first lama in Nepal 1968) to Europe, Australia and North and South America. In Europe he was in charge of the construction of nineteen stupas, among them the highest one outside of Asia at 108 feet. It was inaugurated in Benalmádena in Spain in October 2003, a few weeks after the passing-away of this respected meditation master. The 16th Karmapa said about him: "If I was Buddha, he would be Ananda." (Ananda was Buddha's favorite student.)

Machig Labdrön (1055–1149): Tibetan female accomplisher; often depicted in pale yellow color, dancing, with a double drum in her right hand and a bell in her left hand. She is considered to be the founder of a female Chöd transmission lineage.

Maitripa (1007–1088): Student of Shavaripa, who became a main teacher of Marpa. His core activity was the transmission of the teachings of the Great Seal of the Karma Kagyü lineage. He also taught Marpa the singing of dohas, spontaneous songs of spiritual realization.

Marpa (1012–1097): Known as the "Great Translator." He traveled three times from Tibet to India, where he spent sixteen years learning from his teachers. He was able to reestablish Buddhism in Tibet after it had declined. His main teachers were Naropa and Maitripa. From them he received the Six Teachings of Naropa and the teachings on the Great Seal. He was the first Tibetan lineage holder of the Kagyü school and became the teacher of Milarepa. The transmission for lay people and accomplishers is often called Marpa Kagyü. See also Gampopa.

Milarepa (1040–1123): The main student of Marpa and the teacher of Gampopa, he is the best known of the Tibetan accomplishers. Following his mother's wishes, he took revenge on and killed 35 enemies of his family. Afterward, he sought a way to purify all the bad karma that he had accumulated. He met Marpa and, because of his unshakeable confidence in Marpa and in his own will to meditate even under the most difficult conditions, he reached the realization of the teachings in one lifetime.

Naropa (956–1040): Student of Tilopa and teacher of Marpa; Indian mahasiddha and earlier a scholar of Nalanda University, one of the great Buddhist universities in India. After eight years he resigned from academic life and became a wandering and begging accomplisher, seeking his true teacher. He composed the first written compendium of important tantric teachings, the Six Teachings of Naropa (*Tib. naro chö druk*).

Nydahl, Hannah (1946–2007): wife of Lama Ole Nydahl. Beginning in 1968, she and her husband together studied with the highest Kagyü lamas, among them the 16th Karmapa.

Since 1972 their activities were divided into different fields: She supported the Tibetan lamas and, in doing so, established a very important bridge between East and West. She organized journeys for important Rinpoches and accompanied them, translated important Buddhist texts, gave lectures and supported her husband as he built up centers around the world.

Rechungpa (1083–ca.1160): One of the main students of Milarepa; known as his "moon-like" student. A layman and accomplisher, who was described in the monasteries as the opposite of the ever-virtuous Gampopa, the "sun-like" student of Milarepa. He became one of the teachers of the 1st Karmapa Düsum Khyenpa and stands behind Karma Pakshi in his power-field, which indicates a great honor. He boldly cared for lonesome women.

Sabchu Rinpoche: Main lama of the Swayambhu monastery in Kathmandu in Nepal.

Saraha (late eighth century): One of the so-called mahasiddhas. He was one of the great tantric accomplishers. After getting a female companion, he also worked as an arrowsmith (that is why he is often depicted with an arrow). One of his main statements is that guru yoga is the essence of the "Path of Liberation." He also taught the Essence Mahamudra.

Shamarpa (Tib.) or Shamar Rinpoche: The Red Hat Lama of Tibet (sha = hat, marpa = red). The 2nd Karmapa, Karma Pakshi, announced there would be two rebirths of himself: his own and the one of Shamarpa to secure the Kagyü transmission.

The first Shamarpa Khedrup Drakpa Senge lived from 1283 until 1349. The present Shamarpa Mipham Chökyi Lodrö was born as a nephew of the 16th Karmapa in 1952.

Shariputra: One of the favorite students of Buddha Shakyamuni, born in Nalanda. Buddha sometimes sent students to him who were open for clear insight. His questions again and again challenged Buddha's wisdom. He very profoundly taught the Prajnaparamita Sutra.

Situ Rinpoche (1954–), here the 12th Tai Situ Pema Donyo Nyinje Wangpo: The Khentin Tai Situ Rinpoche belongs to the high-ranking tulku lineages in the Karma Kagyü lineage. His title goes back to the year 1407. The present 12th Tai Situ Rinpoche was born as a son of a farmer in eastern Tibet and shortly afterwards was officially acknowledged as the reincarnation of his predecessor by the 16th Karmapa. He left Rumtek at the age of twenty-two and built up his own place, Sherab Ling, one thousand miles away in northern India's Himachal Pradesh. In 1991 he was the driving force in support of the acknowledgment of Urgyen Trinley, the political candidate appointed by the Chinese, as title holder for the Karmapa.

Tenga Rinpoche (1932–2012): Received profound Buddhist education in the monasteries Benchen and Palpung. He also learned Tibetan medicine. Afterwards he did the traditional three-year retreat. In 1959 he escaped out of Tibet and settled at the main seat of the 16th Karmapa in Rumtek in Sikkim. In 1974 he made his first trip to Europe (together with the

16th Karmapa). Since the early 1990s he has followed the Chinese political Karmapa candidate.

Tilopa (928–1009): Great Indian meditation master and mahasiddha who united the complete transmission of the Diamond Way in himself. He passed it on to his main student Naropa, and thus became the forefather of the Kagyü lineage.

Urgyen Tulku (born in 1920 in Eastern Tibet, died in Nepal in 1996): Holder of both the Kagyü and the Nyingma transmissions. He was not a monk. He founded several monasteries and retreat centers in Nepal. A great lama, well known through books by Lama Ole Nydahl. His book *Blazing Splendor* reveals the complete magic of eastern Tibet and the last Karmapas.

Bibliographical References

Bokar Rinpoche, *Death and the Art of Dying in Tibetan Buddhism*, Clearpoint Press 1994

Chos-Kyi Blo-Gros Marpa, *The Life of Mahasiddha Tilopa*, Paljor Publ. 2002

Chogyam Trungpa, *The Life of Marpa the Translator*, Shambhala Publ. 1982

Ckökyi Nyima Rinpoche, *Das Bardo-Buch*, O.W. Barth Verlag 1998

Clifford, Terry, *Tibetan Buddhist Medicine and Psychiatry: The Diamond Healing*, Red Wheel/Weiser Books 1990

Diamantweg-Stiftung (editor), *Raum und Freude—Space and Bliss*, Buddhistischer Verlag 2004

Doidge, Norman, *The Brain that Changes Itself*, Penguin Books 2008

Dzogchen Pönlop, *Mind Beyond Death*, Snow Lion Publ. 2008

Fenwick, Peter and Elizabeth, *Past Lives*, Headline Book Publ. 1999

Gampopa, *The Jewel Ornament of Liberation,* Snow Lion
Publ.1998

Halcour, Dieter, *Das Lebensrad der Tibeter,* Hanke Verlag 1991

Hodge, Stephen et al., *The Tibetan Book of the Dead,* Thorsons
Publ. 1999

Lopön Tsechu Rinpoche, "*Die Zwischenzustände,*" *Buddhismus
Heute,* 26–30, Part 1–4, 1999–2001

Lyubomirsky, Sonja, *The How of Happiness,* Penguin Books 2008

Nydahl, Lama Ole, *The Great Seal: Limitless Space & Joy:
The Mahamudra View of Diamond Way Buddhism,* Firewheel
Publ. 2011

Nydahl, Lama Ole, *Entering the Diamond Way,* Blue Dolphin
Publ. 1999

Nydahl, Lama Ole, *Ngöndro: The Foundational Practices of Tibetan
Buddhism,* Blue Dolphin Publ. 1990

Nydahl, Lama Ole, *Riding the Tiger,* Blue Dolphin Publ. 1992

Nydahl, Lama Ole, *The Way Things Are,* Mantra Books 2008

Parnia, Sam, *What Happens When We Die?,* Hay House Publ. 2008

Pearsall, Paul, *The Heart's Code,* Broadway Books 1999

Ray, Reginald A., *Secret of the Vajra World*, Shambhala Publ. 2001

Satori, Paula, *The Near-Death Experiences of Hospitalized Intensive Care Patients: A Five Year Clinical Study*, Edwin Melon Press 2008

Sheldrake, Rupert, "The Extended Mind," *Journal of the Society for Psychical Research 68*, 168–172, 2004

Tenga Rinpoche, *Übergang und Befreiung*, Khampa-Buchverlag 1989

Tsele Natsok Randröl, *The Mirror of Mindfulness*, Shambhala Publ. 1989

Thrangu Rinpoche, *Ten Teachings from the 100,000 songs of Milarepa*, Sri Satguru Publ. 1999

Thrangu Pinpoche, *The Spiritual Biography of Marpa, the Translator*, Sri Satguru Publ. 2000

Tulku Thöndrup, *Friedliches Sterben, Glückliche Wiedergeburt*, Windpferd Verlag 2008

van Lommel, Pim, *Consciousness Beyond Life: The Science of the Near-Death Experience*, HarperOne Publ. 2010

Zeilinger, Anton, *Dance of the Photons: From Einstein to Teleportation*, World Scientific Publ. Co. 2008

About the Author

Ole Nydahl was born on March 19, 1941, in the vicinity of Copenhagen. After his service in the Danish Army, he studied Philosophy, English, and German in Denmark, the USA, and Germany. In 1968, on their honeymoon in Nepal, Ole and his wife Hannah Nydahl met great teachers of the Diamond Way for the first time. In 1969 they became the first Western students of the head of the Karma Kagyü lineage, H.H. the 16th Gyalwa Karmapa.

During approximately four years of extensive training in the Eastern Himalayas, they received the most important transmissions and profound teachings of all the former great meditation masters of the Kagyü and Nyingma lineages:

- Mahamudra ("The Great Seal," the highest Buddhist view of the nature of mind) from the 16th Karmapa, 1969–1981
- Kagyü Ngagdzö (the collected "treasures of the most important transmissions" of the Karma Kagyü lineage) from the 16th Karmapa, 1976
- Bodhisattva vows (the inner commitment to devote one's life to the enlightenment of all beings) from Shamar Rinpoche, the second-highest lama of the Karma Kagyü lineage, 1970
- Foundational Practices *(Ngöndro)* by Kalu Rinpoche, 1970–71

- *Kagyü Ngagdzö* from Jamgön Kongtrul Rinpoche, 1989
- Kalachakra ("Wheel of Time" transmission) from Kalu Rinpoche in 1985, Tenga Rinpoche in 1985, the Dalai Lama in 1985 and 2002, Lopön Tsechu Rinpoche in 1994, Beru Khyentse Rinpoche in 2009, and Sakya Trizin in 2010
- Six Yogas of Naropa (advanced Tantric meditation of the Kagyü transmission) from Situ Rinpoche, 1975
- *Phowa* (the practice of Conscious Dying) at the request of Gyalwa Karmapa, from Ayang Rinpoche, 1972
- *Chik Che Kun Drol* (a collection of Kagyü initiations) from Tenga Rinpoche, 1985
- *Rinchen Terdzö* ("Treasure of the Nyingma transmissions") from Kalu Rinpoche, 1983

They also received many other initiations and teachings from the above-mentioned teachers as well as from Dilgo Khyentse Rinpoche, Gyaltsab Rinpoche, Urgyen Tulku, Bokar Rinpoche, Kanjur Rinpoche, Gyaltrul Rinpoche, and others.

In the fall of 1972, the 16th Karmapa sent Ole and Hannah Nydahl back to Europe. They were given the task of teaching and founding Buddhist centers in the Western world in Karmapa's name. Moreover, he authorized the Danish couple to give Buddhist refuge and the Bodhisattva Promise. He first called Ole Nydahl *"Khampa,"* the term for eastern Tibetan warriors. In the following years, when it became unavoidable to take political responsibility for the Kagyü lineage, he was called *"Chökyi Magpön"* ("Dharma-General") and, after some years, he was called "Mahakala," the name of the main protector of the Karma Kagyü lineage. In 1977, in the United States, Karmapa publicly appointed Ole Nydahl as a lama.

The 16th Karmapa remained Hannah and Ole Nydahl's main teacher even after his death in 1981; he connected everything and gives direction to the work until today.

After the death of the 16th Karmapa in 1987, Shamar Rinpoche and Tenga Rinpoche asked Lama Ole Nydahl to pass on the practice of Phowa (Conscious Dying) to Western students. In the same year, Lama Ole Nydahl gave his first Phowa course in Graz, Austria. To date he has transmitted this meditation to more than 90,000 people at an average of twelve courses per year worldwide. He is currently working as the Western expert in the field of life, death, and rebirth, and is also the holder of several Phowa transmission lineages.

In his address to 4,000 participants at a meditation course, Shamar Rinpoche said that the reason that Lama Ole Nydahl's activity continues to inspire thousands of people until today is that he has followed the wishes of his teacher, the 16th Karmapa, precisely and without the slightest doubt.

With undiminished joy and activity, Lama Ole Nydahl is today working closely with the 17th Karmapa Trinley Thaye Dorje, the reincarnation of his former teacher.

Diamond Way
Buddhist Centers Worldwide

A selection of the more than 600 Diamond Way Buddhist Centers of the Karma Kagyu lineage under the spiritual guidance of the 17th Karmapa Trinley Thaye Dorje and directed by Lama Ole Nydahl.

For a complete and updated list of Diamond Way Buddhist Centers and more information, please visit: *www.diamondway-buddhism.org*

AUSTRALIA
www.diamondway.org.au

Buddhist Center Perth
www.diamondway.org.au/centres/perth
Perth@diamondway-center.org

Buddhist Center Sydney
www.diamondway.org.au/sydney
Sydney@diamondway-center.org

NEW ZEALAND
www.buddhism.org.nzca

Buddhist Center Christchurch
www.buddhism.org.nz/christchurch-meditation-centre
Christchurch@diamondway-center.org

CANADA
www.diamondway-buddhism.ca

Buddhist Center Edmonton
www.diamondway.org/edmonton
Edmonton@diamondway-center.org

Buddhist Center Calgary
www.diamondway.org/calgary
Calgary@diamondway-center.org

Buddhist Group Toronto
www.diamondway.org/toronto
Toronto@diamondway-center.org

UNITED KINGDOM
www.buddhism.org.uk

Buddhist Center Exeter
www.buddhism-exeter.org
Exeter@dwbuk.org

Buddhist Center Liverpool
www.liverpool.dwbuk.org
Liverpool@diamondway-center.org

Buddhist Center London
www.buddhism-london.org
London@diamondway-center.org

IRELAND
www.diamondway-buddhism.ie

Buddhist Center Dublin
Dublin@diamondway-center.org

UNITED STATES OF AMERICA
www.diamondway.org

Buddhist Center Albuquerque
www.diamondway.org/albuquerque
Albuquerque@diamondway-center.org

Buddhist Center Austin
www.diamondway.org/austin
Austin@diamondway-center.org

Buddhist Center Chicago
www.diamondway.org/chicago
Chicago@diamondway-center.org

Buddhist Center Houston
www.diamondway.org/houston
Houston@diamondway-center.org

Buddhist Center La Crosse
www.diamondway.org/lacrosse
Lacrosse@diamondway-center.org

Buddhist Center Los Angeles
www.diamondway.org/la
LosAngeles@diamondway-center.org

Buddhist Center Madison
www.diamondway.org/madison
Madison@diamondway-center.org

Buddhist Center Maui
www.diamondway.org/maui
Maui@diamondway-center.org

Buddhist Center Miami
www.diamondway.org/miami
Miami@diamondway-center.org

Buddhist Center Minneapolis
www.diamondway.org/minneapolis
Minneapolis@diamondway-center.org

Buddhist Center New York
www.diamondway.org/ny
NewYork@diamondway-center.org

Buddhist Center Portland
www.diamondway.org/portland
Portland@diamondway-center.org

Buddhist Center San Diego
www.diamondway.org/sandiego
SanDiego@diamondway-center.org

Buddhist Center San Francisco
www.diamondway.org/sf
SanFrancisco@diamondway-center.org

Buddhist Group Santa Fe
www.diamondway.org/santafe
SantaFe@diamondway-center.org

AUSTRIA
www.diamantweg.at

Buddhist Center Vienna
www.diamantweg.at/wien
Wien@diamondway-center.org

BELGIUM
www.bvdd.be

Buddhist Center Brussels
www.bvdd.be/centres.html
Brussels@diamondway-center.org

CZECH REPUBLIC
www.bdc.cz

Buddhist Center Prague
www.bdc.cz/praha
Prague@diamondway-center.org

DENMARK
www.buddha.dk

Buddhist Center Copenhagen
www.buddha-kbh.dk
Copenhagen@diamondway-center.org

GERMANY
www.diamantweg.de

Buddhist Center Berlin Mitte
www.buddhismus-berlin-mitte.de
Berlin-Mitte@diamondway-center.org

Buddhist Center Hamburg
www.buddhismus-hamburg.de
Hamburg@diamondway-center.org

Buddhist Center Munich
www.buddhismus-bayern.de/muenchen
Munich@diamondway-center.org

Buddhist Europe Center
www.europe-center.org
join@europe-center.org

HUNGARY
www.buddhizmusma.hu

Buddhist Center Budapest
www.buddhizmusma.hu/budapest
Budapest@diamondway-center.org

MEXICO
www.budismo-mexico.org

Buddhist Center Mexico City
www.budismocondesa.com
MexicoCity-Condesa@diamondway-center.org

POLAND
www.buddyzm.imail.pl

Buddhist Center Warszawa
www.stupahouse.pl
Warszawa@diamondway-center.org

RUSSIA
www.buddhism.ru/eng

Buddhist Center St. Petersburg
www.petersburg.buddhism.ru
Petersburg@diamondway-center.org

SPAIN
www.budismo-camino-del-diamante.es

Buddhist Retreat Center Karma Guen
www.karmaguen.org
KarmaGuen@diamondway-center.org

SWITZERLAND
www.buddhismus.org

Buddhist Center Zürich
www.buddhismus.org/zuerich
Zurich@diamondway-center.org

VENEZUELA
www.budismo-camino-del-diamante.org

Buddhist Center Caracas
Caracas@diamondway-center.org

Other Books by Lama Ole Nydahl

BUDDHA & LOVE

Timelesss Wisdom for Modern Relationships

Buddha & Love explores all aspects of love and partnership from a Buddhist perspective. Covering a broad spectrum of topics such as sexuality, infidelity, parenting, and divorce, Lama Ole Nydahl explains how a Buddhist approach to relationships can help us to relax our minds, break bad habits, and use relationships to grow ourselves and benefit everyone around us. Unafraid of taboo topics, and free from sappy cliches and political correctness, Nydahl provides modern people with practical advice on how to love better.

Translations: English, German, Bulgarian, Polish, Spanish, Russian, Czech, Hungarian

ISBN-13: 978-1937061845

ENTERING THE DIAMOND WAY
Tibetan Buddhism Meets the West

This is the genuinely compelling story, and spiritual odyssey, of Ole and Hannah Nydahl, who in 1968 became the first Western students of the great Tibetan master, His Holiness the 16th Gyalwa Karmapa. Their exciting travels led them to experience the skillful teachings of numerous Tibetan lamas who helped transform their lives into "limitless clarity and joy." The aim in writing this book is "to form a bridge between two worlds, and especially to share with all who are looking for their true being ... an introduction to a time-proven way to Enlightenment."

Translations: English, German, Danish, Polish, Russian, Hungarian, Dutch, Italian, Spanish, Czech, Lithuanian

ISBN: 978-0-931892-03-5, 2nd edition

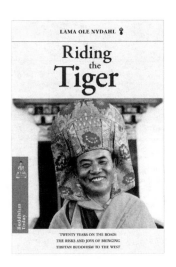

RIDING THE TIGER

Twenty Years on the Road: The Risks and Joys of Bringing Tibetan
Buddhism to the West

In 1972, after three years of intensive meditation practice in the
Himalayas, Lama Ole Nydahl and his wife, Hannah, began teaching
Buddhism in Europe at the request of H.H. the 16th Gyalwa Karmapa.
Riding the Tiger is the inside story of their experiences bringing
Tibetan Buddhism to the West.

Translations: English, German, Polish, Russian, Spanish, Dutch, Hungarian

ISBN: 978-0-931892-67-7, 2nd edition

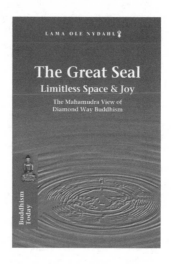

THE GREAT SEAL
Limitless Space & Joy:
The Mahamudra View of Diamond Way Buddhism

Lama Ole Nydahl's refreshing and modern commentary to this classic Buddhist text about the nature of mind makes these teachings accessible to many people. The Great Seal describes our basis for development, the path, and the goal of Diamond Way Buddhism and offers insight into both the conditioned world and absolute reality. The Great Seal, or Mahamudra view, is the experience of here and now, beyond expectations or fears, without holding on or pushing away.

Translations: English, German, Polish, Spanish, Danish, Hungarian, Russian, Czech, Finnish, Bulgarian, Dutch, Greek

ISBN: 978-0-9752954-0-3

THE WAY THINGS ARE
A Living Approach to Buddhism for Today's World

More than a Buddhist textbook, *The Way Things Are* is a living transmission of Buddha's deep wisdom, given by a Western Buddhist master. In this contemporary text, Lama Ole Nydahl provides an overview of Diamond Way Buddhism for modern people looking to incorporate Buddhist practice into their daily lives.

Translations: English, German, Danish, Russian, Ukrainian, Serbian, Bulgarian, Finish, Swedish, Lithuanian, Czech, Slovakian, Hungarian, Dutch, Spanish, Japanese, Polish, Italian, Croatian

ISBN: 978-1-84694-042-2, 2nd edition